I

THE GREATEST
GOLF SWING

Also by Philip Reed

Nonfiction

Candidly, Allen Funt

Free Throw: 7 Steps to Success at the Free Throw Line

Fiction

Bird Dog

Low Rider

The Marquis de Fraud

In Search of the
Greatest
Golf Swing

Chasing the Legend of Mike Austin,
the Man Who Launched
the World's Longest Drive
and Taught Me to Hit Like a Pro

Philip Reed

Carroll & Graf Publishers
New York

In Search Of The Greatest Golf Swing
Chasing the Legend of Mike Austin, the Man Who Launched the World's Longest Drive and Taught Me to Hit Like a Pro

Carroll & Graf Publishers
An Imprint of Avalon Publishing Group Inc.
245 West 17th Street
11th Floor
New York, NY 10011

Copyright © 2004 by Philip Reed

First Carroll & Graf edition 2004

All rights reserved. No part of this book may be reproduced in whole or in part without written permission from the publisher, except by reviewers who may quote brief excerpts in connection with a review in a newspaper, magazine, or electronic publication; nor may any part of this book be reproduced, stored in a retrieval system, or transmitted in any form or by any means electronic, mechanical, photocopying, recording, or other, without written permission from the publisher.

Library of Congress Cataloging-in-Publication Data is available.

ISBN: 0-7867-1366-6

Designed by Simon M. Sullivan
Printed in the United States of America
Distributed by Publishers Group West

For Mike Austin, who helped me,
and so many other golfers.

CONTENTS

CHAPTER 1

THE 300-YARD BARRIER

On a beautiful winter day in 1997, I pulled up in front of a golf course in Studio City, California, with two friends. We parked and walked by the putting green, crowded with golfers quietly stroking putts who, like myself, were dreaming of someday shooting that perfect round of golf. We entered the Spanish-style clubhouse, under towering eucalyptus trees, and walked into the pro shop.

"I'm looking for Mike Austin," I said to the guy behind the counter. "He said you could tell me where to find him."

"Mike Austin," the guy repeated. "If Mike isn't teaching right now, he's sitting under the big tree just to the right of the first tee."

I thanked him and we walked back outside. Sure enough, I could see a man, his back turned toward us, sitting at a table near the first tee box. Even from this distance, I could see he was a big man with powerful shoulders. His brilliant white hair gleamed in the sunlight. I approached and circled around so I could see his face, and he mine, as I addressed him.

"Mike Austin?" I asked, just to be sure.

"Yes, sir," he answered in a strong voice with a hint of a Scottish burr.

"I'm Phil Reed."

"The writer."

"That's right. It's good to meet you."

When I offered my right hand, Austin grasped it with his left. At first I thought this was odd, but then I remembered he had suffered a stroke some years ago and was paralyzed on his right side. His hand was cool, but his grip was quite strong; I felt I was touching steel. This brief physical contact was coupled with a penetrating gaze from his pale blue eyes, which were undimmed by age. As I stared into his eyes, an uncomfortable feeling stirred inside me. I felt I was being appraised, as if Austin was gauging my size, my strength, and somehow, my masculinity. That quick, withering stare inspired in me a feeling of uneasiness that I would often experience in his presence.

Although I knew Austin had to be in his late eighties, his face was remarkably young for a golfer who had spent so many years in the sun. His skin was, of course, lined. But he was still a handsome man with rugged features. On his upper lip he sported a pencil-thin mustache. His snow-white hair was combed straight back, and there was a set to his jaw as if he were holding something firmly between his front teeth. The result gave his face an animal snarl, like a predator ready to pounce.

"Excuse me for not getting up, sir," Austin said, still gripping my hand. "Since my stroke, my movement has been limited."

"Mike, I'd like you to meet my friends," I said, stepping back. "This is Jim Ullrich, from Conroe, Texas."

"Pleased to meet you, sir," Jim said in his characteristic twang.

"And this is Dr. Tom Amberry," I said, ushering my other friend forward. "Tom holds the Guinness record for making more consecutive free throws than anyone in history."

The challenging gaze that Mike had trained on me disappeared as he looked at Dr. Tom. It was replaced by a profound look of respect.

"It is a great pleasure to make your acquaintance," Austin said humbly. "I've read about your record—you've accomplished a truly remarkable feat. You should be very proud."

"Hot dog!" Jim said. "Two Guinness champions in one place! How often does that happen?"

"Please, sit down," Austin said, indicating the seats across from him at the rough wooden table.

We chatted for a moment, explaining how, coincidentally, both Jim and I had read a recent golf magazine article about Austin and decided to contact him.

"I was comin' out to visit Phil here," Jim said, "And I thought, shoot, I could get my book signed by two world champions at the same time."

Jim produced his hardbound edition of the *Guinness Book of*

3

Guinness *champions Dr. Tom Amberry (left) with Mike Austin.*

World Records and opened it to Dr. Tom's listing, where it described how he had made 2,750 free throws in a row over a twelve-hour period. He was seventy-one when he performed that feat. And he never did miss—they were closing the gym, so he was kicked out. Tom signed below his entry in the book in a round, graceful handwriting. Jim admired the autograph for a moment and slowly turned the book to Austin. With some difficulty Austin gripped the pen in his left hand and slowly, shakily, began to sign his name. It took some time to do this, and as he labored over it in silence I read the entry I had read so many times before but could still hardly believe:

The greatest recorded drive on a standard course is one of 515 yards, by Michael Hoke Austin of Los Angeles, CA, in the U.S. National Seniors Open Championship at Las Vegas, NV on September 25, 1974. Austin drove the ball to within a yard of the green on the par-4 450-yard fifth hole of the Winterwood Course and it rolled 65 yards past the flagstick.

I looked across to the nearby driving range, where dozens of golfers were hitting balls. There was the usual variety of swings: impatient slashes; tentative swipes; loose, looping pinwheels. One man's swing was so panic-stricken it looked like

Mike Austin

■ Longest drive

The greatest recorded drive on a standard course is one of 515 yards, by Michael Hoke Austin of Los Angeles, CA, in the U.S. National Seniors Open Championship at Las Vegas, NV on September 25, 1974.

Mike Austin's Guinness *entry, signed by the man himself.*

he was trying to kill a snake with his club. The results of these swings were equally mixed: topped shots, worm burners, snarling hooks, and wild slices that zoomed off the range. After hitting a shot, one golfer would curse and slam his club down onto the mat. Then, wearily, he would begin this routine again. He would tee up another ball, hit it, curse, and then pound the mat. In short, it was a typical sampling of golfers who were struggling for consistency and distance. What was it, I wondered, that made this game at once so addictive and yet so diabolically difficult?

My own game had come a long way in the eight years that I had been playing. I began by shooting around 100 thanks to some God-given athletic ability and an analytical nature. But once I decided to take the game seriously—to actually try to improve—my scores shot up as high as 110. I began to read golf instructional books, most of which did little more than add to my confusion and hurt my scores. Eventually, I came to form a rather low opinion of most golf teaching. But by playing once a week and practicing, I was able to bring my score back below 100 and then break 90. Now, I was shooting in the mid to low 80s. Of course, my goal now was to break 80. But to do that, there was one thing I lacked—distance. I rarely hit my drives more than about 200 yards. My 7-iron went only about 130 yards.

Distance is the dream that every middle-aged golfer chases. And the pursuit of distance is what brought me here today, for

I was, at this moment, sitting with the man who had set the record for driving a golf ball farther than any other human being. Ever. Let me take a moment to put this accomplishment into perspective. Tiger Woods, the greatest golfer of our time, once said that his longest drive was 415 yards. He said he hit that drive while he had been playing a practice round before the British Open—and was assisted by a wind that was howling at his back. Mike's drive, at 515 yards, was a whole football field longer. Furthermore, Austin had unleashed that prodigious blast at the age of sixty-four, with a steel-shafted, persimmon-headed club rather than the titanium clubs and hot golf balls used by Tiger. Clearly, Mike's swing must be different to get such an amazing result. I wanted to discover what Mike's method was for obtaining such incredible distance on his drives. I wanted to learn his secret to improve my own golf game, but I also wanted to describe it in a book that would help other struggling golfers.

"Mike," I heard myself saying. "Do you think you could teach someone like me, someone my size, to hit the ball three hundred yards?"

I expected another appraising stare from Austin. I expected him to ask how tall I was, or to question my strength, or to qualify his answer in some way. Instead, he quickly answered, "Distance has little to do with size or strength. Distance comes from supple quickness." As he said those magic words, "supple quickness," he cocked his left wrist, tucked his shoulder

U.S. NATIONAL SENIOR OPEN

1974

LAS VEGAS, NEVADA

MIKE AUSTIN, PRO

NEW WORLD RECORD DRIVE

515 YDS.

One of the many awards hanging on Mike's living room wall.

slightly, and made a fluid swinging motion. And in that small, deft motion, I saw a faint echo of his greatness. It was like handing a baseball to a Hall of Fame pitcher and seeing his old, gnarled fingers work into just the right grip to throw a slider or a curve.

"You see that net out there?" Mike pointed at the backstop for the driving range, which was at least 150 feet tall. "I had a student, a young woman, after taking lessons from me she was hitting the ball *over* that net."

As he said this I felt my mind expanding. It was like I had just glimpsed a new me—or what I could be with the right coaching and lots of practice. I had experienced this sensation before, when I first met Dr. Tom and saw him shooting free throws for an hour and never once missing. As Dr. Tom worked with me, and I began making long, unbroken series of baskets, I felt my mind grasping the idea that I was—and all athletes are—capable of far more than I ever imagined. As Dr. Tom said in his book (which I cowrote), *Free Throw: 7 Steps to Success at the Free Throw Line,* "We are more limited by our beliefs than our abilities."

We talked for quite awhile as we sat under that tree next to the driving range. The topic was mainly golf, since both Jim and I were anxious to soak up as much of Mike's wisdom as we could. From time to time, Dr. Tom chimed in with observations about how athletes could perform successfully in clutch situations, such as shooting a free throw with the game on the line.

9

I couldn't help thinking how good I would be if I could combine Mike's power golf with Dr. Tom's knowledge of performance under pressure. The time passed quickly, and it was only hunger that reminded us it was well past noon. We agreed to adjourn to a local restaurant.

As we drove through midday traffic I reflected on our conversation. I was excited to have met someone like Mike who had the expertise to teach me how to gain the distance I craved. At that moment, I made a decision to commit to learning the Austin swing. I would stop the silly experimentation I had been using to find my golf swing and dedicate myself to learning what had made Mike such a prodigious hitter. I decided I would set aside my goal of breaking 80 and replace it with a new one: I wanted to hit a 300-yard drive while playing a round of golf on a regulation course.

I set this goal of a 300-yard drive even though I knew I would be wildly happy with consistent drives on an average of 250 yards. But the round figure of 300 yards set a clear benchmark that captured my imagination because it was so easy to visualize. Certain even numbers become obstacles that are more difficult to achieve. Dr. Tom had told me that many people struggled to make, say, ten free throws in a row. They keep missing on their ninth shot. But once they make a perfect ten in a row and set their sights higher—on twenty, perhaps— then they keep missing on the nineteenth.

Now, my goal was to be standing 100 yards farther down the

fairway when I hit my second shot. If I could hit the 300-yard drive, my second shot would typically be with a wedge. Or, like Mike, maybe I would drive the green on short par-4s. What would I have to do to gain those extra 100 yards? I would have to enter Mike Austin's world—the world that at once intrigued and intimidated me. Little did I know as I began that journey that I would learn about so much more than just golf. Or that I would gain so much more than a more powerful golf swing.

CHAPTER 2

THE GREATEST SWING EVER

Over lunch at a local restaurant, in the shadows of the nearby movie studios, we listened as Mike launched, unprompted, into stories of his exploits over the years. He seemed eager to impress us with his larger-than-life accomplishments. According to the tales he told, he had spent much of his life fighting off challengers who were either trying to beat him in organized sporting events—on the golf course, or in the boxing ring—or in sudden violent clashes in bars, locker rooms, or back alleys. While Austin was always a tournament golfer and professional instructor, he also took on all those who challenged him to any kind of a bet or contest.

One story involved a midnight telephone call from somewhere deep in South America back in the 1930s. A promoter there had discovered a Mexican golfer who could blast enormous drives and was sure the gentleman could outhit Austin. The next day, Austin was on an airplane heading south. Arriving in Mexico thirty-six hours later, without any sleep, Austin found himself paired with a club pro in a high-stakes match against the long-driver and the great Argentine golfer Roberto De Vicenzo (who was denied a playoff in the 1968 Masters Tournament when he signed an incorrect scorecard). Austin not only outdrove the challenger but won the match and collected well over $10,000 on the bet. He was amazed when he realized they had been playing for American dollars, not Mexican dollars, worth ten times more at the time.

In another story, Mike told us how he had run a driving range in Culver City for many years. One night, three college football players snuck in and tried to steal golf balls from him. When he confronted them, they all rushed him. He fought off the first two, then nailed the third man with a punch so powerful it drove his jawbone back into his face and he began choking to death on his own tongue. Mike had to grasp the shattered jaw and pull it back into position so the unconscious man could breathe. The other two, seeing this, turned tail and ran.

I was skeptical of some of these stories and was a bit put off by Austin's boasting. On the other hand, as a writer who is always looking for good material, I had to admit it was colorful and compelling stuff. While I found one part of my mind trying to debunk and reject these yarns, another side of my mind said, "Yeah, but if it's true . . ." In Austin's anecdotes it always seemed he was leaving a trail of beaten golfers and bloodied victims. Then, suddenly, Mike leaned forward, and with a devilish gleam in his eye and a conspiratorial growl to his voice, he told us a dirty joke.

Our explosion of laughter brought a faint smile to Mike's lips.

But it was a challenging smile, as if to say, "Okay, what have you got?" He leaned back, waiting. Luckily, I always have a joke handy for just such a moment. I told my joke, and at the punch line Jim and Dr. Tom cracked up. Looking across the table, I was pleased to see Mike smile and nod, as if to say, "Okay. Not bad." I felt I had passed a test—swapping dirty jokes with real men.

We left the restaurant and agreed to follow Mike back to his home in Woodland Hills, in the San Fernando Valley, about twenty miles north of Los Angeles. Despite the 1989 stroke he suffered, which would have put a lesser man in a wheelchair, Mike moved without a walker or even a cane. He had devised a way of standing erect and swinging his paralyzed leg forward. While this may make him sound freakish, he certainly wasn't. Mike was still a proud, imposing figure. Walking with a ramrod-straight spine and a countenance befitting royalty, Mike slowly strode toward his gigantic, white 1982 Cadillac Biarritz. Tom, Jim, and I followed behind in my car, watching Mike thread his way through traffic on the 101 freeway with a wrist draped over the steering wheel, smaller cars seeming to scatter like tenpins in his wake as he plowed through them.

Turning off the main road, I found that Mike lived on Irondale Avenue—which seemed very appropriate for a golf legend. It made me think of the fictitious character Chivas Irons in Michael Murphy's classic novel *Golf in the Kingdom*. Would Mike become my own Chivas Irons, a difficult but enlightening teacher? We pulled up in front of a modest, fifties-style tract home on the corner of the block. A second old Cadillac was parked in the drive. As we walked to the front door, I noticed a rubber golf mat with a groove worn down the middle of its green synthetic grass. An aluminum chair was placed beside the golf mat. I didn't know it at the time, but this is where Mike gave most of his lessons.

We stepped through the front door and I found myself in a dark, narrow hallway. As my eyes adjusted to the gloom, I saw the wall was covered with framed photographs of golfers and celebrities, each one signed with warm regards to Mike Austin. I recognized Arnold Palmer, Seve Ballesteros, and even fitness guru Jack La Lanne. On a living room wall were sequence shots of a golfer wearing a straw hat.

"Who's this?" I asked Mike.

He looked at me, surprised, and simply said, "Snead."

Mike stood beside me for a moment, and I saw his sharp eyes dart from picture to picture throughout the sequence shots of Sam Snead, as if turning the staccato photographs into a fluid swing. Clearly, he was checking the positions at each stage of the swing, assessing it with an expert's eye. Then, in a soft voice, again filled with the admiration I had heard when he talked about Dr. Tom's record, he said softly, almost reverently, "Now that's a beautiful swing."

"You ever play with Slammin' Sam?" Jim asked.

"Hell, yes," Austin replied. "I beat him four and two at Riviera and he wouldn't even shake my hand. Another time, at the Tam O'Shanter, he saw me hit an eight-iron two hundred ten yards and back it up twenty feet. He said, 'Christ, how can you play this game in two directions at once?' "

Mike's claim made me think of how average golfers work so hard to spin the ball enough so that their wedge shots back up even a foot or two. Now, Mike was telling me he could back up an 8-iron 20 feet. It was, I thought, another claim that seemed to defy reality. But I also thought how it must have given Mike an incredible advantage to stop the ball on hard greens or to shoot at "sucker pins" that were tucked near a sand trap.

We moved into the small living room, and directly ahead of me I saw a large Barcalounger. This was Mike's chair. It faced a big-screen television set with a stack of videotapes on top. Reading their titles, I saw they were all golf instructionals. More golf photographs were on the walls, many of them sequence shots of Mike's swing throughout his life. In one set of photos he wore a contraption around his neck, a swing trainer he later told me he had invented called "The Flammer." There were also plaques honoring Mike's golfing achievements and long-drive contests. One plaque named him the Southern California Golf Professional of the Year in 1984, and another from *Golf Digest* named Mike one of the ten greatest teachers in the country in 1991. Among all these awards I found a hand-lettered page, framed and mounted on the wall, titled "The Spine." Reading the text, which I quickly realized were Mike's own words, I found it was a description of how the spine moves during the golf swing. In it, he called the legs the "power" of the golf swing and the wrists the "accelerators."

Mike demonstrates his swing trainer, "The Flammer."

Mike's Barcalounger was like the cockpit of a jet fighter. Around this central position were all the tools of his trade. He had a phone and a fax machine, the remote for the television and VCR, and a Rolodex from which I would later see him pull the names and numbers of many golf greats and longtime legends. In addition, he had within easy reach a 7-iron, a driver, and a putter. He had anatomical charts, which he used to show students the correct position of the muscles and bones, and an odd selection of items that he used to illustrate different swing principles, such as a tire iron from a car.

Leaning against the walls of the dark living room were sets of golf clubs and putters, many of which were designs that I'd never seen. One putter had a Plexiglass head with a prism embedded in it. I picked it up and put it behind a golf ball that was lying nearby. By looking down at the putter head you could see over the ball and toward the target.

Seeing my interest in the club, Mike said, "Paul Runyan designed that."

"Paul Runyan," I echoed, recognizing the name as a golf champion of the 1930s and '40s. "I read a great book by him on chipping and pitching."

I might have imagined it, but I felt an icy chill from Mike's

10   Part III/Sunday, May 13, 1984 ★ ★

Golf / Shav Glick

Mike Austin, 74, Is Southland PGA Pro of Year

Mike Austin, at age 74 still one of the world's longest hitters, is 1984's Southern California PGA Golf Professional of the Year.

Although the powerfully built Austin, who teaches kinesiology as it applies to the mechanics of the golf swing, may have lost a few yards off his drives through the years, he remains a member in good standing of the 350 Club, made up of big hitters who regularly reach such distances in competition.

Austin is in the Guinness Book of Records for the longest drive in tournament play—a prodigious 515 yards during a U.S. National Senior Open at the Winterwood golf course in Las Vegas.

A life member of the PGA, Austin lives in Glendale and is affiliated with the Studio City course as a teaching professional. He was once head pro at the Moonridge (now Goldmine)

Mike's teaching brought him widespread recognition.

direction. *Professional jealousy?* I wondered. "The man was a short-game wizard, but a very short hitter. If I could have putted half as well as Runyan, I would have won every tournament I entered," Mike snarled.

"What do you mean?" I asked, a little taken aback by his sudden admission.

"I hit every fairway and every green in regulation. Even my chipping was great. But on the greens I was hopeless."

It was the old "drive for show, putt for dough" story. Although hitting the long ball put a golfer in scoring positions, it all came to nothing if you couldn't put the ball in the hole. The galleries love to see Tiger hit long drives, but it is his superior putting—particularly under pressure—that has won him so many tournaments. Even with sub-par putting skills Mike was able to win 128 tournaments including the 1978 U.S. National Open Senior Championship.

"The other players and the press, they were always giving me the needle about my putting," Mike continued. "One sports writer said, 'If you want to see the most marvelous thing *and* the most pitiful thing, watch this howitzer on the tee and this motorboat on the green: putt, putt, putt.' I had so much adrenaline for the long drive that when it came to putting I would line up the ball and then, *bam,* hit it right off the green. The only thing I could do to control it was to hypnotize myself. I did that for the Long Beach Open in 1960 and beat Lloyd Mangrum to get into the final."

"Long Beach," I said, surprised. "That's where I live. My home course is Recreation Park."

"That's where the tournament was held."

Finally, I thought, among all Mike's claims, here was something I could verify. My wife was a librarian for the Long Beach Public Library, and she could find a record of this in the archives of the local library. I made a mental note to check on this tournament later.

I picked up one of the clubs Mike had leaning against the wall. It was a 1-iron with a rather small head. Instead of the popular cavity back, this was more of what was once called a "muscle back" design, with extra weighting behind the sweet spot. "Who makes this?" I asked.

"That's one of mine," he said. "All these manufacturers, they don't have any idea of the physics behind the golf swing. They make the driver heads hollow. I put a tungsten rod right behind the sweet spot. I took it to a tournament and let the pros demo it on the practice range. They were coming up to me *begging* to buy it—at any price."

Again, I felt my "B.S. meter" going off. All of Austin's stories seemed to end in some self-aggrandizing statement. It was odd to me that this late in life he still felt so eager to prove himself.

"Mike," I said. "I know you've told it a million times, but I have to hear it directly from you. Can you tell us how you set the world record?"

He fixed me in a steady gaze, his head cocked, as if

challenging me to doubt him. Then, in a low rumbling voice he began.

"It was the second day of the National Seniors Open in Las Vegas. I was playing in a foursome with Chandler Harper, who had won the PGA Tournament, Pete Flemming, and Joe Brown. I was hitting the ball a ton that day, even for me. I reached two of the par-five holes with a driver and a seven-iron. They needed to hit a driver, *a three-wood*, and a seven-iron. Finally, we came to the fifth hole, a flat four hundred fifty-yard par-four. Harper said to me, 'Mike, you've been knocking the hell out of the ball today. Let's see what happens if you really let one rip.' They passed the word up to the group on the green that was still putting and told them I was going to go for it.

"I was using a Wilson persimmon-headed driver with a forty-four-inch, extra-stiff steel shaft and a one-hundred-compression golf ball. I took my usual swing at it, but all along keeping the green as my target. You see, I didn't swing any harder—I just told myself I wanted to hit it to the green. Hell, I felt I was just swinging at cruising speed. The ball took off and went up about twenty feet. But instead of following a parabolic curve, it flattened out. I've never seen anything like it. It just held its line, staying up in the air. It finally hit on the fringe of the green, bounced over, and rolled sixty-five yards past the flagstick. I pitched back on the green and three-putted for a bogey."

We all laughed, but Jim articulated our thoughts: "Greatest

drive of all time and you walk off with a bogey. Drive for show, putt for dough."

"How old were you at the time?" I asked.

"Sixty-four," Mike replied, leveling his challenging gaze at me that always seemed to say, *Wanna make something out it?*

"Was it windy?" I asked.

"There was a twenty-five-mile-per-hour tailwind."

"Was it downhill?"

"Level."

He had heard all these questions before, from skeptics who wanted to believe it was all rigged, eager for a way to diminish his accomplishment. Dr. Tom told me he got the same type of question from players who doubted his record. Did he use a regulation basketball? Was the basket larger? Did he really shoot from the foul line?

We were quiet for a moment, each of us interpreting Mike's story in our own way. I don't think I really believed it. After all, it was unprecedented, a quantum leap beyond anything else. I knew that the biggest hitters on tour averaged only about 300 yards. Professional long-drivers could swat it 350 and occasionally 400 yards. But they lifted weights, hit juiced-up balls, used long-shafted drivers, and probably took steroids.

"Is there a secret?" I asked. "Is there something you know that the others don't? I mean, how do you explain this?"

He was about to answer when a new voice, a woman, spoke to us from the darkness of the hallway: "I was there at that tournament. I saw it with my own eyes. It was like God held the ball in the air."

She took a step forward and we saw an attractive woman in her sixties, with intense eyes. Her black hair and large earrings made her look a bit like a gypsy fortuneteller. She was dressed in golfer's clothes and had a glove tucked into the back pocket of her slacks.

"Gentlemen," Mike said, "my wife, Tanya."

We all introduced ourselves. Then, Mike turned to her. "What did you shoot?" he demanded.

"Four over. I won the tournament."

"Four over? Christ, woman! What happened?"

"Mike, I won the tournament. Okay?"

"But four over?"

She turned her back on him and disappeared into the kitchen. Moments later, she reappeared with a tray of soft drinks.

I wandered over to a rack of golf clubs, selected one, and took my address position. "Mike, on the wall over there, I was reading what you wrote about the spine. You say that the legs provide the power and the wrists are the accelerators. What is the leg action you recommend?"

"I don't *recommend* any leg action," he said. "There is only one way to use the legs properly if you want to get the ball out there."

"Okay, what is it?"

24

"Begin with sixty percent of your weight on your back leg, forty on your left. Make a forward press as you begin to transfer your weight forward, then back. As you swing the club back . . ."

I began trying to follow his instructions. Suddenly I heard what sounded like a shotgun blast.

"No, sir!" Mike bellowed. "Don't back the hip up!"

I tried to rectify the action.

"NO!" he roared again. "Not that way! Christ, in that position you couldn't hit a bull in the ass with a bass fiddle. Bend the left knee! Point the knee at the ball as you—"

I felt my face growing red. It took me back to my school days when a sadistic math teacher would call me to the blackboard to solve problems as she ridiculed me in front of the class. I wanted to just put the club down and walk away. But Mike was fighting his way out of the chair, raising himself with the help of a cane he kept nearby. He lurched toward me. As I gripped the club, he gripped me, twisting me this way and that as he barked instructions and knocked my knee into position with his cane. Finally, he was pleased with the results.

"Yes, sir!" he exclaimed. "Now *that's* the compound action of the pivot."

I held the position, relieved. A short time later I escaped to the safety of the sofa, sipping a Coca-Cola provided by Tanya, who smiled sympathetically at me as if she understood all too well how I felt. I let the others talk, my face burning and my ears echoing with Mike's angry words. Eventually, we excused ourselves by saying we had to take Jim to catch a plane back to Texas. We all said good-bye, and the three of us climbed back into my car.

On the drive back to the airport, Jim said, "Well, Phil, there's your next book."

"I'd never survive," I said, still stinging from losing a wrestling match to a half-paralyzed old man.

"I thought he was going to kill you," Dr. Tom said. "He had you in a full Nelson and a headlock all at the same time."

"Hell, you can put up with that," Jim said. "It's history! Someone has to get this down on paper."

A few days later, my humiliation had ebbed and was now replaced by curiosity. I went to the Long Beach Public Library and looked up the 1960 tournament Mike had described. My expectation was to find that he was only another name in the field. With the help of my wife, Vivian, I threaded the micro-film for the *Long Beach Press Telegram* into the reader. I watched as headlines from four decades ago whirled past my eyes. I found the date and moved to the sports section. A bold headline greeted me: "MIKE AUSTIN JOLTS MANGRUM, BATTLES HOLSCHER FOR TITLE." I sat there stunned. My first thought: *He wasn't lying.* My second thought: *I wonder if the other things he told me were also true.*

The lead paragraph of the story read: "For the love of Mike (Austin's hypnotized putter), there were a pair of bonnie fine upsets on the links at Recreation Park Saturday." Later on in

PART OF HUGE GALLERY AT RECREATION PARK SATURDAY WATCHES MIKE AUSTIN (A

SUNDAY
Sports
Independent-Press-Telegram

SUNDAY, JULY 10, 1960   Page C-1

Mike Austin Jolts Mangrum,
Battles Holscher for Title

By JERRY WYNN
For the love of M i k e (Austin's h y p n o t i z e d putter), there were a pair of bonnie fine upsets on the links at Recreation Park Saturday!

Mike Austin, playing in a state of p a r t i a l self-hypnosis, stunned mortal Lloyd Mangrum, 4 and 2, and Bud Holscher shot unconscious-type six-under par golf to jolt mere four-under man Eric Monti, 2 and 1, in semifinals of the $9,000 Southern California PGA Championship.

Thus all that remains to-day of the pre-tournament f i r m of Mangrum, Monti and Money is the . . . ter . . .

$1,800 to the winner and $1,000 to the runnerup in the morning at 9:30 and afternoon at 1:30.

Austin, full professor at the Mike Austin School of Golf in Hollywood a n d assistant professor at the Institute of Infinite Science in L.A., said he was hypnotized twice by fellow pro Ed Hamilton during the week and again after he beat Bob Roux on the 19th hole in Saturday morning's quarter-final round.

"It definitely is the reason f o r my s u c c e s s," claimed the 6-foot-2, 205-pound strongman who long has been known as a colorful performer because of

his l o n g-hitting prowess and flamboyant character, but who never before has been a serious title threat.

"I could always hit the ball as good or better than

Saturday's Results

QUARTERFINALS: Mike Austin def. Bob Roux, 19th hole; Lloyd Mangrum def. Dale Andreason, 3-1; Eric Monti def. Ralph Evans, 4-3; Bud Holscher def. Red Wiley, 2-1.
SEMIFINALS: Austin def. Mangrum, 4-2; Holscher def. Monti, 2-1.

the next golfer, but I would lose out chipping and putting. I was so bad on the greens that the other golfers would call me Motorboat . . . putt, putt, putt.

"Now Ed has my inhibitive nerves blocked through hypnosis. My fears are re-laxed. I can putt with confidence."

School will remain out on Austin's mental powers until today, for his putting Saturday while good f o r him was far from sensational. In fact, a miss of an 18-inch tap on the 17th hole against Roux, almost cost him that match.

It followed a 1 5-f o o t birdie putt by the promising young Irvine Coast CC pro, and instead of victory for Austin, the match was even. Mike won the 19th by driving to the b a c k fringe of the green on the 308-yard first hole and holing out in two putts for a b...le.

Against Mangrum, who played well (two under) in ousting Dale Andreason, 3 a n d 2, in t h e morning, Austin parlayed his o w n stout t w o-under shooting with a few costly putting lapses by his tiring opponent i n t o the startling victory.

Mike beat the legendary Lloyd Mangrum to get into the finals.

the story, the writer described Mike as "the 6-foot-2, 205-pound strongman who long has been known as a colorful performer because of his long-hitting prowess and flamboyant character." A photo of Mike holding up his putter read, "No yip, with hyp" alluding to the fact that Mike had apparently beaten the dreaded putting yips—twitchy mishits that send the ball shooting past the hole—by using hypnosis.

Sitting in the quiet of the library, I was transported back to 1960 as I turned the pages and read about the conclusion of the tournament on Sunday. For a moment, I actually felt I was reading that morning's paper, not already knowing the outcome. "A match that started with the bizarre aspect of a hypnotized golfer, Mike Austin, ended with a fantastic comeback as Bud Holscher won four of the last five holes (and sank a 28-foot putt to halve the other)."

Much of the publicity centered on the fact that Mike had been hypnotized. The sports writer referred to Austin as "zany," a "Joe pro," and "a character," and seemed biased against him. The writer seemed delighted to relate that Austin lost the tournament and had walked off with his head bowed. But then came this interesting sentence: "Moments after losing, Austin was seen amusing the gallery by demonstrating his no-hands rope trick."

I thought of Austin's story of flying to Mexico to outdrive the local big hitter. I thought of Jim's exhortation that I write about Mike's historic accomplishments. I thought of what it would feel like to hit a 300-yard drive. I picked up the phone and dialed. It was answered on the first ring.

"Mike Austin," came the strong voice with the hint of a Scottish accent.

"Yes, Mike. This is Phil Reed. I met you the other day with Jim and Dr. Tom."

"Yes, sir. It was a pleasure to meet you."

"Thank you. I found a newspaper story of that tournament you told me about at Recreation Park Golf Course. I can fax it to you if you'd like."

"I would be very grateful if you would, sir. My house burned down in the seventies, and I lost all my clippings."

"I've got your card with your numbers on it. I'll fax it in a few minutes. And I'd also like to buy your Flammer and your instructional video."

He took down my ordering information for the Flammer and his video called *Golf Is Mental Imagery*. We talked for a few more minutes, even though I still felt uncomfortable recalling how he had turned me into a pretzel while giving me that golf lesson. Still, just before I hung up, I couldn't help asking one more question: "What was your 'no-hands rope trick'?"

CHAPTER 3

ON LEARNING GOLF

When I met Mike Austin, I was a self-taught golfer. I had never had a golf lesson and had developed my swing based on reading books, looking at pictures in magazines, and getting tips from my playing partners. In other words, I learned the game in the same way that most people learn it—patched together from various sources and filtered through my own sensory system. Like so many other golfers, I would occasionally—and probably by accident—hit a great shot. I would watch the ball in flight, holding a straight line toward the center of the green, and think, *Why can't I do that every time?*

I'm not one of those guys who has fond memories of playing golf with his father. Though my dad taught me to play tennis and other sports at a young age, he often told me golf was a waste of time, a sport for fat old men. However, he thought hitting balls at a driving range was great fun, as if all the pleasure of the game could be squeezed into this one acceptable activity. I remembered how Dad would load us all into the station wagon and drive out to the range on a hot summer night.

We would get a club—any old club—from the pro shop and flail away, launching little white streaks through the light and into the darkness beyond. When I was about twenty years old my younger brother, Peter, a great athlete who loved games of all kinds, got his own set of clubs. We split the bag (I took the odd-numbered clubs and Peter used the evens) and we played nine holes now and then.

Some years later, while working the night shift as a police reporter for the *Rocky Mountain News,* in Denver, Colorado, I golfed several mornings a week with a friend from the paper. For the first time, I actually began to make an effort to improve. I remember how one morning a homicide detective I knew from covering the police beat was waiting to tee off behind us. I wanted to unleash a big drive to impress him, to show him I was a real man too, so I took a huge cut at the ball. The result was a wild slice that took off sideways and nearly killed a woman three fairways over. *What a weird sport,* I thought, retrieving my ball and apologizing profusely. *The harder you try, the worse you play.* I put my clubs away and turned my back on golf again for a long stretch.

Five years later, I found that golf—at least talking about it—was a good way to communicate with my father-in-law. He was a big, silent Southerner who worked nights for the railroad in Richmond, Virginia, so he could spend his days on the golf course. Once, to make conversation, I asked him why golfers cut divots in the grass when they hit iron shots. Without answering, he disappeared into his garage and returned with a wedge and a handful of balls. He threw the balls down on his front lawn and began hitting shots into the woods across the street.

"You have to hit down on the ball," he said, cutting a fat divot out of his own lawn. "Hit down on the ball, then take the divot." He demonstrated again and another long strip of turf was cut from his lawn. But he wasn't worried about his grass. He was admiring his wedge shot, the ball jumping off his club and soaring over the trees across the street. "Puts backspin on the ball—makes it check up on the green," he explained.

A year after retiring from the railroad, my father-in-law was diagnosed with lung cancer. He never got a chance for all the golf he dreamed of playing in retirement. He died at home, in a bed by the window, looking out at the rain-blackened trunks of leafless trees in the late winter. We flew into Richmond for the funeral, and I noticed his golf bag in the corner of the garage. It was the loneliest sight I ever saw. His set of clubs was missing the putter, though, since it was going to be buried in the casket along with him. I guess he wanted it just in case they do play golf in heaven. My father-in-law had known, as all golfers did, that once you find a putter that puts the ball in the hole, you never let it go. Ever. The rest of my father-in-law's clubs were divided between his two sons, Brad and Wilson.

A short time later I began playing golf myself, as if the baton had mysteriously been passed from my father-in-law to me.

This time around, I decided I would really improve; I would study and learn to play this difficult game.

In 1996, the year before I met Mike Austin, I was looking for a subject for a sports book. A friend of mine had wisely suggested I pick subjects for books that I myself wanted to learn about. In this way, he said, "They'll be paying you to learn." I examined my interests and quickly found golf. I began looking for the subject of a golf book and a way to write about my newly adopted sport.

Instead of finding a golfer to write about, however, I stumbled across a story about Dr. Tom Amberry, a seventy-three-year-old Long Beach, California, man who had made 2,750 free throws in a row to enter the *Guinness Book of World Records.* I met "Dr. Tom" a short time later and proposed writing a book with him about free throw shooting. At first, I couldn't wrap my mind around Dr. Tom's accomplishment. But as I researched the book and began shooting free throws, and improving more than I ever thought possible, I began to explore two fascinating concepts: performance under pressure and how an athlete expands the limits of his or her abilities.

I was surprised to find that while writing the book on free throw shooting, my golf scores dropped significantly. This was because my short game (chipping, pitching, and putting) improved thanks to Dr. Tom teaching me his methods of "focus and concentration." My drives weren't any longer, my irons still lacked the sizzle I was looking for. But with the consistency I had learned at the free throw line, my scores steadily dropped.

There was, however, a game within a game at which I was still the loser—the long drive. In golf you can bogey every hole, and lose every skin, but if your tee shots are longer than your partners', you are *the man.* This was Mike Austin's world. And I wanted to get in on the action. When I hit a drive, I wanted my partners to whistle and say, "That's huge!" Instead, I'd quickly put away my club after hitting, not wanting my partners to see what iron I used from, say, 150 yards. When I hit my tee shot on a par-3, I dreaded the immediate chorus of shouts from my foursome: "Short!"

My secret agenda, my reason for willingly suffering the abuse Mike heaped on his students, was to join the elite club of long hitters. I'll just come right out and admit it—I wanted to be a real man. And what better instructor to teach me than Mike Austin? He wasn't just the longest of the long. He had boxed and fought and gambled and won everything he did in his life. Besides that, he had already promised that my stature wouldn't be a hindrance. At five feet, eight inches tall, I could never come close to matching Mike pound for pound. But I knew I could achieve his indispensable quality of supple quickness.

One of the gifts I was endowed with was my athletic ability. I was never big or strong or brave, nor was I ever the top student in the class. But I excelled at sports and won the admiration of my teammates by helping our side win. Sports became my passport to acceptance in the early years of my life. At forty-five years old, when I first met Mike, I was still in good shape. On the tennis court I could easily run down shots other players didn't try for. On weekends I played goalie in a coach's soccer league, and my stamina was good enough to help me make it to the summit of Mount Whitney four times—a twenty-two-mile round-trip hike that I did in one day.

A week after my first visit with Mike, his video and swing trainer, the Flammer, arrived in the mail. I had been eagerly awaiting them and put on the Flammer right away. It was a black disk, about the size of a CD, that is held over the sternum with straps that criss-crossed behind the back. On the disk there was a ball-and-socket joint that connected to an adjustable rod that held the very end of the golf club's grip. It was as if this rod connected the club to the center of your chest. Consequently, if your torso turned, the club moved too. Furthermore, the rod held the club in an exact radius around the body. With the club held by the rod, I could relax my grip on the club and feel the "supple quickness" that Mike had described.

With the Flammer strapped to my chest I felt a bit like the Kevin Costner character in *Tin Cup*, who uses every imaginable golf training aide to try to cure his ailing swing. Actually, the Flammer was one of the devices pictured in the movie. I popped in the video and, still wearing the Flammer, took my stance in front of the TV. I saw a younger Mike Austin, in his seventies perhaps,

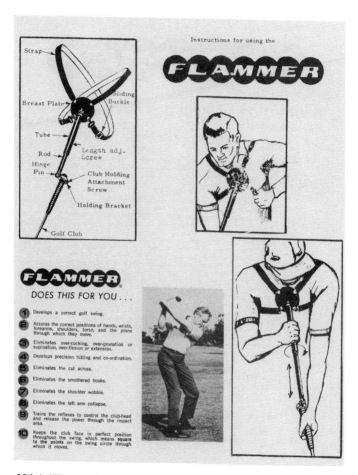

Mike's "Flammer" was seen in the golf movie Tin Cup.

LAKELAND LEDGER

SPORTS

12   LAKELAND LEDGER,

FLAMMERS AID SLAMMERS

Kinesiology Promotes Sweeter Swing

By CHARIE ROBERTS

Applied kinesiology will never replace Harold Sargent, Harry (The Hat) Walker and their ilk as teachers of the correct way to strike golf balls and baseballs.

But it may keep them awake nights trying to spell it, and it probably will help them tremendously in developing more faultless techniques in their proteges.

A mechanical aid called the Flammer, recently invented in California by native Atlanta golf professional Mike Austin, has led some top baseball batting instructors and golf pros, including Sargent, to embrace that theory.

Kinesiology, the study of principles of mechanics and anatomy in relation to human muscular movement—and related corrective exercises — led in development of the revolutionary Flammer, one for golf, another for baseball.

And Sargent, who recently has been employing the device personally and in his instruction of golfers at East Lake Country Club—as have other pros here and elsewhere — says, "Some gadgets aren't much good, but this thing has real merit. It's the best instructional aid I've seen."

Meanwhile, Austin has been lecturing and helping baseball people in Tigertown at Lakeland, Fla. employ the baseball Flammer in an attempt to correct flaws in batting swings of young and old Tigers in Detroit's spring training camp.

"It's impossible for a batter to 'hitch' while harnessed in the Flammer and swinging a

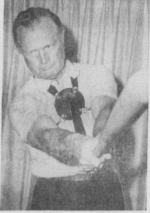

Staff Photo—Hugh Stovall
MIKE AUSTIN JOINS HIS OWN SWING SESSION
It's Baseball Here, But Atlantan's Device Helps Golfers, Too

bat held firmly by the arm which projects from a breast plate," said Austin on a recent visit here. "And Detroit teaching personnel have expressed great pleasure with results there so far in training."

"This is the best thing ever to come along for golf instruction," says Sargent. "Best

thing about it is that it holds the club face so that it can't open or close throughout the swing.

"Too, the arm of the Flammer fixes the radius of the swing so it can't be increased or decreased. It forces the left arm to remain extended the same distance through the backswing, downswing and

through and after contact with the ball.

"I've tried swinging my club for five minutes while harnessed in the Flammer, then five minutes after taking it off. I retain the same 'feel' with the same muscular reflex. I'm getting good reaction from it with pupils too."

"Proper sequence of action, co-ordination, getting the proper feel, and correcting poor swinging positions and habits—both in golf and baseball—is the idea," says Austin of the 'swing trainer' he illustrates in an accompanying picture.

"We have found that the Flammer assures correct position of hands, wrists, forearms, shoulders, torso and the plane through which they move. It also eliminates over-cocking, over-pronation or supination, over-flexing and extension."

BE A TRACTOR-TRAILER DRIVER

Learn a Skill Worth Real Money to You

Over-the-highway freight carriers are searching for professionally trained tractor-trailer drivers. Only skilled men can qualify for these high-paying jobs . . . just wanting one isn't enough. But chances are, if you are 21 or over and can drive an automobile, and have the spirit and initiative necessary to be a professional driver on a highway freight rig, we can help you make the grade. For complete information without obligation, write giving your name, address, age, and telephone number to National Professional Truck Driving, 817 Healey Bldg., Atlanta 1, Ga. or call 688-2004.

The Flammer was also used by baseball players.

white-haired with a pencil-thin mustache and wearing a sporty straw hat. In the background, I recognized the golf course where I had first met Mike sitting by the first tee box. In the video, shot in the mid-1980s, Mike teaches a young woman to play golf. She is tall and athletic, a statuesque beauty with a long, graceful swing and a full-balanced follow-through.

But it was the beginning of the video that really caught my attention. In it, Mike is putting on an exhibition for a crowd that enthusiastically cheers each shot. It was the first time I had seen Mike's swing, and there was something about it that I hadn't noticed in any pro's swing I had seen on television. Since I knew of Mike's world-record blast, I expected some awesome display of power. Instead, I saw a precise, graceful swing that launched the ball on an identical trajectory every time. The more I watched Mike's swing, the more I realized it had a unique quality that almost defied description. Finally, I put my finger on it. Although the brute force I expected was missing, I saw laser-beam intensity as he came down into the hitting area. All his motions were highly focused at the moment of impact, precise and economical, yet blended with fluid grace. I thought of his description of his world's record: "I felt like I was swinging at cruising speed." I watched his swing over and over and began to feel that all the power in his body was transferred from his hands, down the shaft, and into the explosive flight of the golf ball.

Another interesting element of the video was that Austin demonstrated some of his trick shots. He began by hitting

NORTH HOLLYWOOD · STUDIO CITY · TOLUCA LAKE

Daily News
Neighbors Wednesday, August 14, 1985

10-SE

He's 74, but Austin still drives the ball like a record holder

By GREGORY J. WILCOX
Daily News Staff Writer

Michael Hoke Austin had been belting the ball pretty well all day. So when he stepped on the tee at the 450-yard, par-4 fifth hole at the Winterwood Golf Course in Las Vegas, his playing partner, Chandler Harper, also a pretty fair ball striker, proposed a challenge.

Austin had reached some par-5 holes with a driver and 7-iron.

mail a long par-4 hole? "Oh, no. I've hit over a hell of a lot of par-4 holes," he said at Studio City Golf and Tennis, where he gives lessons.

Austin, 74, is 6 feet 1 inch tall, weighs a solid 205 pounds and has a visitlike grip. There isn't a green anywhere he doesn't think he can reach in one or two shots.

But once on the putting surface Austin becomes mortal. He can cover 500-plus yards in two shots, then sometime take twice

❝ I was never a good putter ❞
— Michael Hoke Austin

a task usually requiring three shots. "Harper said, 'Mike, you're hitting the ball extremely well. Let's see how far you can hit it,'" Austin recalled. "I hit it right on the screws."

The ball rose into the air, rode a 35-mph tail wind, bounced within a yard of the green and rested 65 yards beyond the putting surface, 515 yards — nearly half a mile — from where Austin and some astonished onlookers stood.

That prodigious poke is the longest drive recorded on a regular course and landed Austin, a Glendale resident, in the Guinness Book of World Records.

What is even more remarkable is that Austin was not one of the young lions on the PGA Tour. He was 64 at the time and competing in the 1974 U.S. National Seniors Open Championship.

He gives basically the same answer when asked to explain the monstrous shot: The ball simply defied the law of physics and was held in the air by God.

Was Austin surprised to air-

as many strokes to negotiate the final 30 feet to the hole.

"I was never a good putter," he says in a voice still laced with the lilt of his native isle of Guernsey.

In 1954, Austin was hit in the face by a golf ball and lost sight in his right eye for a year. When sight was restored his right eye was lower than the left, and from then on all the greens looked like the deck of a listing ship.

Nevertheless, Austin has earned a comfortable living from golf. He has managed to take time out for some of life's other pleasures, like flying small airplanes in Africa during World War II, singing opera and acting. His latest acting job was that of Judge Lang in the movie "The Star Chamber."

He also travels the world giving unusual golf clinics. Austin wears a skeleton suit to demonstrate how the body's muscles and bones function during a golf swing.

Please see AUSTIN Pg. 3

Inside

Michael Hoke Austin conducts a golf clinic while wearing a skeleton suit. He says he uses the suit to demonstrate how the body's muscles and bones function while making a swing.

Mike wore a skeleton suit to show the proper positions during the swing.

normal iron shots. Then he hit the same shots with just his left hand and then just his right hand. Then he turned the club over and hit the shot left-handed but with the toe of the iron's blade pointed down. Every time, the ball soared straight as an arrow.

Looking at Mike's face as he was hitting balls, I saw that he had an intense grimace. I took this to be a product of his concentration. But it was much later that I learned the reason for his expression. "I had just recovered from a serious accident and was in excruciating pain," Mike said, describing the accident that happened in 1984. "I was at a stoplight when a truck rear-ended me. I was thrown through the windshield and across six lanes of traffic. After that, I was in constant pain and couldn't teach for six months. I had to relearn the golf swing all over again. I could do it, but it filled me with unbearable pain."

At the tail end of the video was footage taken in the 1960s from "The Mike Austin Golf Show," which aired in Los Angeles on KHJ-TV. It featured Mike dressed in a black leotard with the bones of a human skeleton painted in white on the suit. As he explains his method you can see where the bones of the body should be during the golf swing. It was a very different approach to golf instruction, and at the time, it must have seemed very high-tech, if a bit bizarre with its ghostly effect.

After working with the Flammer and studying Mike's video, I began to realize that if I wanted more distance I would have to use my lower body much more aggressively. Most golfers, myself included, are nearly paralyzed from the waist down.

"The
Mike Austin
Golf Show"

KHJ-TV, in its vein of "Sports
Spectaculars", invites you to a most
unique exhibition of golf instruction
with MIKE AUSTIN, a "Class A" member
of the PGA with 35 years of experience
in exhibiting, instructing and playing
professional golf!

This show is an entirely new approach
to teaching golf via the medium of
television and is the second in its
series. AUSTIN will explain the stance,
control, proper grip, correct way to
address the ball, and will demonstrate
the part that the feet, knees and legs
play in the total swing. He accomplishes
this by wearing a suit painted to show
the various muscles and bones in the
human body. Under black lighting, you
see just the outlined anatomy in action,
enabling the viewer to see each movement
the particular part of the body makes
for a successful golf swing!

Through the use of slow motion film,
the viewer is also shown the smallest
detail regarding conventional shots
(from the wedge thru the driver) and some
of MIKE AUSTIN's famous 'trick' and
variety shots.

This show is bound to be another KHJ-TV
'sports bonanza'....as with its chain of
of 'spectaculars' such as FLOYD PATTERSON
STORY (11.0) SURFBOARD CHAMPIONSHIPS (6.0
BASEBALL (13.0) BASKETBALL (20.0) earning
double-digit ratings* and in each case the
#1 INDEPENDENT in the time-period.

See.... M I K E   A U S T I N
"World's Longest Hitter in Golf"

KHJ-TV Channel 9

For additional information
contact: KHJ-TV or
RKO General Natl. Sales

*Special ARB coincidental on request

On his golf show, Mike once drove a golf ball through a phone book.

This lack of motion is probably an attempt to control the shot
more closely. Watching Mike's swing, I saw that his hips swung
like a bell below his rock-steady head. His left heel came well
off the ground on the backswing, while his right heel came up
and that foot turned over on the follow-through. Much later, he

told me that if the right heel is kept on the ground through the downswing, "you're dragging a dead man." Furthermore, keeping the right heel on the ground promotes a twisting motion that will eventually injure the spine.

I practiced the advice in the video and swung the Flammer every day and began to feel myself improving. I was eager to try out my new swing on the course. I had hit balls on the range, and the contact felt crisp. But it was hard to tell if the shots flew farther than before. So I played a round with my regular foursome at Recreation Park, where Mike had battled Lloyd Mangrum in 1960. The first hole is a downhill dogleg right, with a city street running along at the foot of the hill behind a chainlink fence. For my first tee shot, I focused mainly on my legs, flexing my left knee and letting the club move back and then up into position. At the top of the backswing I flexed my right knee and let my weight shift. This slid my hips toward the target, lowered my right shoulder, and brought the club onto the correct plane. The contact was solid, and I looked up to see a low, bullet drive that split the fairway. It hit and rolled through the dogleg and wound up against the fence.

"Whoa," one of my partners said. "That's too much of a good thing."

It wasn't a showy drive, one of those shots that climbs into the sky, hangs there, then falls lazily back to the ground. It was a line drive, and as old-time golfers say, "it was as straight as a string." It traveled about 250 yards—my longest drive at that time.

Mike puts on a demonstration at Recreation Park circa 1939.

All that day, I was hitting low, driving tee shots. I was out in front of my partners after most of my drives. On one hole, a 360-yard par-4, I hit it up and over a rise and caught the down slope. Previously, the closest I had ever been to this hole after my tee shot was 150 yards. After that drive, I hit a wedge from 90 yards. I was so close to the hole I didn't know how to play it and took a bogey.

Recreation Park clubhouse as it looks today.

As I walked off the course that day, I was confident I had learned something I would never forget. While my hands did little more than hold the club, my legs turned my torso and put my shoulders on the right swing plane. I felt I could come out anytime and simply generate power with my legs to hit a 250-yard drive. I'd take that any day.

Unfortunately, the sensations I felt that allowed me to hit those drives evaporated by the next time I played. My shots flew right, then left, then straight up in the air. I lost my confidence. The Austin video lay on my shelf unwatched. The Flammer gathered dust in the corner of my garage. These were the outward signs of my problem. But the true problem was invisible. It was in my mind. I had once again accepted

45

inconsistency and mediocrity. But there was a glimmer of hope for me, because I had done it once and therefore I knew that I could do it again. But unless I could return to my short-lived good form, the more pressing question was, how could I ever reach my 300-yard goal?

It was time to swallow my pride, to admit that the teacher-student contact—no matter how humiliating—was the greatest way to learn. I would go visit Mike again, get my swing straightened out, and try to understand what had made him the longest of the long hitters. If I could fathom Mike's accomplishments, and learn his secrets, maybe I could make some sparks of my own.

CHAPTER 4

THE GOLFING BANDIT

"One of the editors here was talking about that old golfer who was in the *Guinness Book of World Records*. Would you be interested in writing a piece about him for the magazine?"

It was my friend Martin Smith, a senior editor for the *Los Angeles Times Magazine,* contacting me out of the blue. The call came just as I was going to see Mike Austin again and begin, in earnest, to learn to hit the long ball. I had recently taken a full-time job at Edmunds.com, the consumer-oriented automotive Web site, and I didn't have time to play a lot of golf. But I had decided I still had time to pursue my goal of learning to hit the long drive. Now, here was a golden opportunity: fulfill my dream, obey Jim Ullrich's exhortation to chronicle Mike's golfing achievements, and get paid for doing it.

"Marty, I'm going to write an article about Austin that will be the best-read piece in the magazine—ever." I was amazed at my own brash words. I was beginning to sound like Mike, claiming to be the best at anything I did. "I mean, how can you miss with a piece like that? Every guy who isn't golfing on a Sunday morning will at least want to read about golf."

"What I had in mind," Marty said, "was to make it like a *New Yorker* piece and really go into detail about the physics of the swing. Then you need to describe what other golfers do—and get Austin to describe what he does that is so different and so much better."

"He can definitely do that," I said. "But he's also got this amazing background that I've only begun to learn about."

"Weave all that in there," he said. "You've got a lot of room. So go for it."

Yes, I definitely would *go for it* in more ways than one.

A week later, I was sitting in a restaurant in the San Fernando Valley with Mike Austin and my friend Dr. Tom Amberry. I took Dr. Tom with me for self-defense, since I knew today's meeting with Mike would include a golf lesson. I asked Mike to give me a free lesson, for purposes of the article, to see how quickly he could help me improve. He rose to the challenge, saying, "Bring your seven-iron and I'll get your swing in shape." I thought that with Dr. Tom there Mike might not manhandle me quite as much—and I would be able to absorb more of what he taught.

We were waited on by a beautiful young woman with raven hair, translucent alabaster skin, and a stunning figure. Mike's eyes seemed to glow every time she came to our table. According to her nametag she was "Graziella."

"Is that Greek?" Mike asked her.

"Italian."

"Italiano," he said. "*Parla Italiano?*"

"Only a little."

"*Dammi un bacio,*" he said to her and I saw her cheeks redden. Then in English: "Do you want that translated?"

"No, that's one phrase I've heard a lot," she said and hurried off.

I recognized the key word in the phrase and said to Mike, "Why didn't she want to kiss you?"

"You know Italian?" he asked, chuckling.

"No. But I figured it out. How many languages do you speak?"

"I can get by in Spanish, and I speak Italian, Greek, and some Russian. Of course I took Latin in school and used that quite a lot when I was studying medicine. My favorite language is Greek, though. It's much easier to do mathematical calculations in that language. And after a11 while I found it was easier to think in Greek."

I didn't quite know how to react to this, since English was the only language I had ever spoken fluently. I struggled with French in school and, during a brief Hemingway phase, traveled in Spain and learned enough Spanish to make train connections and order in a restaurant. It blew my mind to think of having command of enough languages where you could choose the best one to think in. I wanted to reject this statement, but I was learning that Mike's claims were never hollow. And what was that bit about "studying medicine?" I could see that I had a lot to cover.

It was time to get started with the interview. I turned on my tape recorder and said, "I need to get some biographical information about you. Then we're going to talk about the golf swing. And then if your offer of a lesson is still open, you can make an experiment out of me."

"I'll get you hittin' the ball out of sight in no time," Mike said, looking around for the waitress again.

"So, Mike, let's begin at the beginning. When and where were you born? What was your family like? Let's talk about how you grew up."

Mike sat back in the booth and began to describe his early years, so long ago. He was born on the Isle of Guernsey, one of the two Channel Islands off the coast of England, on February 17, 1910. Michael Hoke Austin was the youngest of five—he had two brothers and two sisters. When I asked him if any of them were still living, he replied, "No, sir, I'm the last of the Mohicans."

Mike's father, Sir Joseph Lafayette Austin, was the head chemist for the Imperial Chemical Company. He was an imposing figure who wore a Homburg hat and spats and would catch a ferry on his way from the Isle of Guernsey every Monday morning to his office in London, not to return until Friday night. According to Mike, his father had developed the most powerful poisonous gas ever formulated. The British were going to use it against Germany in World War I, but it was so deadly it would have made a desert of the landscape. The generals were afraid that if they unleashed it in Germany it would drift back across the English Channel and decimate the British Isles. Eventually, the deadly substance went unused and they sealed it in stainless steel tanks and dumped it in the North Sea.

Mike's mother was American, descended from Robert E. Lee. She was an accomplished pianist as well as lead soprano for London's Royal Opera . In the early years of Mike's life, he accompanied her on trips and listened as she sang in the greatest opera houses in Europe. Later, she gave voice lessons and taught Mike to sing well enough that he would later sing professionally.

When Mike was about six years old, he had his first golf lesson. His father leased a nearby golf course and decided Mike should be sent to the local pro, a man named Callahan, for lessons. It had just rained, so the course was closed and, Mike speculated, the pro was more interested in getting the youngster out from underfoot than he was in giving him a complete lesson. He eyed Mike over the counter in the pro shop and suddenly thrust a club at him.

"Take this mashie niblick, and I want you to bury the head of the club in that wet bank out there," he pointed to a nearly vertical bank of exposed dirt near the clubhouse. Then he leaned over the counter and glared at the boy. "But if you come back here with any mud on your sleeve, I'm going to kick you right in your rump."

51

Mike did as he was told. Years later, he realized the exercise was the greatest lesson he could have ever been given. It taught him to release the head of the club with a throwing action rather then pulling the club through the hitting area with his hands and arms. To avoid muddying his sleeve, he had to accelerate the clubhead so that it moved faster and traveled out ahead of his hands at the moment of impact. The drill replicated the effect of hitting an "impact bag" used by some teaching pros today. Learning to release the club, Mike said, became the basis of his long-hitting prowess.

"You'll never hit it a long way by pushing the club through," he said. "You can't get it out there by pulling the club through, understand? But you can throw it a long way. That's how you hit the long ball."

The Austins moved to Grenoch, Scotland, when Mike was about ten years old. By this time he was playing golf as often as he could. The family then prepared to move to the United States in 1921 and boarded the *Aquitania,* the sister ship to the *Lusitania,* which was torpedoed and sunk by German U-boats during World War I. They landed in New York harbor and moved to Massachusetts, where Mike's mother gave voice lessons at Boston University.

A few years later, Mike's father was driving through Boston when his car was struck by a trolley and dragged several hundred feet. He was hospitalized for months, and eventually the family moved again, this time to Florida, hoping the change of climate

As a teenager, Mike's drives impressed golf legend Bobby Jones. Mike is pictured here, circa 1935, in the balanced finish that characterized his swing.

would speed his recovery. Now a teenager, Mike was set upon by the local boys, attacked for being a foreigner and a Yankee. This was less than fifty years after the Civil War, yet the regional hatred between North and South was still festering. Furthermore, Mike's hair was almost white (he was like an albino except for his blue eyes), which incited the other boys to taunt him.

"The sons of bitches ripped me apart," Mike recalled. "Every day they called me 'angel,' 'iceberg,' 'snowball'—anything to insult me. I got in a lot of fights, and the principal thought I was the meanest son of a bitch she'd ever had in her school. She didn't know that I just didn't want to take that shit. I had to stay in class until everyone else had left school, because I was injuring the other kids.

"Finally, I told my father, 'These kids are jumping on me in gangs. You can't watch all the sides of a circle.' My father said, 'We'll put a stop to that.' He put me in a local boxing school. After that, I beat every son of a bitch that insulted me if I caught them alone. I broke their jaws, their noses, and knocked their teeth out. I hated to tear their faces up, but I did. I had a very hot temper after that. If you nag on a dog every day, he'll turn mean."

The hot Florida sun nearly burned Mike's skin off, so he begged his mother to seek another home. They looked around and finally chose Atlanta, Georgia, because it was a little cooler and because, according to the chamber of commerce, it had the best water in the United States. They moved in to a house across the street from the East Lake Country Club, where legendary golfer Bobby Jones practiced under the guidance of the Scottish pro Stewart Maiden.

Mike used to sneak onto the golf course to hit balls, and one day Maiden caught him. But instead of punishing him, he told Mike, "Son, there's no need for you to slip in here. You have a very good swing and I don't want to hinder your progress. I'm going to allow you to play here during the week after school. But if you come on Saturday or Sunday, I'm taking away your privileges. You can use my practice balls as long as you wash them and put them back."

The practice range at the East Lake Country Club allowed Mike a refuge during his stormy teenage years. He worked on his swing every day and eventually began hitting the ball so far he could fly it across a lake that was near the range. To do this he had to hit the ball 300 yards—which was unheard of in those days when a good drive, for a pro, was about 250 yards. One day Bobby Jones stopped his lesson with Stewart Maiden to watch Mike hitting the ball across the lake. He came over and said, "Sonny, how do you do that?" Mike told him, "Sir, you're taking a lesson from Mr. Maiden. He's a professional. I'm just an amateur. You ask him—he'll tell you."

At the age of eighteen, Mike turned pro and began playing in tournaments. Some of the other golfers he knew on the Professional Golf Association (PGA) tour were Paul Runyan (who was about five years older than Mike), Tommy Armour, and Gene Sarazen. He quickly became known as the tour's longest hitter but discovered that this distinction made him a pariah. When he went to a city to play a tournament, he always found himself relegated to the tee times saved for the "dew sweepers"—golfers teeing off at first light, while the fairways were still wet with dew. He couldn't figure out why he was always given these undesirable early morning tee times instead of being grouped with the well-known players who teed off later, when spectators showed up to watch. One day he learned the answer.

"In Kansas City, I came out to play and I found myself paired with a player who was in the top ten," Mike recalled. "I asked him, 'How did you get the bad luck of having me for a partner?'

"The player said, 'I don't pay off.'

" 'What do you mean by that?' I asked him.

" 'The PGA commissioner setting up the tournament is taking payments from the other pros so they don't have to play with you.'

"I was amazed. I asked, 'What do I do that they don't like? Do I step on their line?'

" 'No.'

" 'Do I talk while they're hitting?'

" 'No, no,' the player said. 'They don't want to be embarrassed. You hit the ball so far, you make them feel they are playing in the foursome behind you.' "

At the next general meeting of the PGA, which was held in Chicago, Mike brought a complaint about the commissioner who had been accepting bribes from the other players not to be paired with him. The man had been head of the PGA tour for twenty years and had just bought a new house and had children in college. But after Mike's accusations, he was removed. Reflecting on this story, Mike added, "Everyone who's ever tried to double-cross me has either died or something bad has happened to them. I feel I'm blessed in a way."

In those early days of professional golf, a pro couldn't make a living on tournament winnings alone, because the prize money was so low. To supplement his winnings, Mike turned to gambling and developed impossible-sounding shots and bet other players he could make them. For example, he would throw a ball in a sand trap, step on it so just the top of the ball was visible, then bet someone he could get "up and down in three"—with a driver. He had discovered that by hitting behind the ball, with the edge of the club, he could explode the ball out of sand. Then it was an easy two-putt—even with Mike's subpar putting—to ice the bet.

Dr. Tom, who had been listening carefully as he ate his lunch, particularly enjoyed this story. He told us that after setting his free throw record, basketball players often challenged him to shooting contests. He kept a one-hundred-dollar bill in his wallet to deal with these types. Whenever he was approached in this way, he pulled out the bill and told them to match his stakes if they wanted to bet. The sight of that much money usually discouraged most challengers.

While playing golf tournaments, Mike continued his education at Emory University and Georgia Tech, studying engineering and physics. He planned to eventually become a doctor. But one day, while viewing an operation in a local hospital, he suddenly passed out. It turned out that he was allergic

to ether, so he abandoned his plans to continue studying medicine. However, he had progressed far enough to get a sound
background in anatomy, which, years later, would help him
analyze and perfect the golf swing.

Meanwhile, Mike had honed his gambling skills to the point
where his exploits became fodder for the gossip columnists
and sports writers across the South. From 1929 to 1933 he was
known in the newspapers as the "Golfing Bandit." Every winter
Mike would turn over the Atlanta golf shop he was running to
his assistant and head south into Florida. He visited the golf
courses from Jacksonville to Pensacola and told the pros there,
"I'm a PGA member and I'm a gambler. I'll play anybody for
any amount of money. Set up some matches for me and I'll give
you a cut of my winnings."

Most of Mike's opponents were gangsters from the northern
cities who were spending the winter months in Florida. They
loved to gamble and were quick to challenge Mike to a high-
stakes game. But after Mike beat them soundly the first year,
they wouldn't take his action the following winter. Mike
bought a set of left-handed clubs and challenged them to a
match in which he had to play left-handed, his opponents not
knowing that Mike was actually ambidextrous. He still won,
even though they would further handicap him by stepping on
his ball or kicking it into the rough. The next year Mike had to
play one-handed to get a game. "But I still skinned them," he
chuckled, taking a sip of his coffee.

Beating the gangsters was one thing, but collecting their money was another. Some of his opponents carried machine guns in their golf bags. When Mike tried to get his money, one thug told him, " 'You try to take my money, I'll shoot your hands off.' I figured I needed my hands, so I got the hell out of there," Mike recalled.

The most elaborate hustle Mike pulled off was when he bet a local businessman ten thousand dollars that he could make par hitting the ball with a Coke bottle. He taped the bottle so it wouldn't shatter and then developed a swing where he would crouch beside the ball and hit it off a high tee. He got to the point where he could hit the ball nearly 200 yards in this fashion. A large group of spectators came out to see the bet settled, and when Mike made good on his claim it was written up in the local papers. The course he was running back in Atlanta was city-owned, and after his boss read about his exploits in the local papers, Mike was told his actions reflected poorly on the city. He was advised to either give up the gambling life or lose his job.

Using the skills Mike developed as a hustler, he took his act on the road and performed trick shots in front of crowds assembled for baseball games or county fairs. An impresario would travel several weeks ahead of Mike to drum up interest for him and an archer who did trick shots with a bow and arrow. Mike would amaze audiences with a variety of shots. "I would turn the ball right, then left. Then I'd hit a low shot that rose up and went over the fence. Then I'd hit what we called a 'parachute shot' that would fly high and slowly fall back to the ground. Then I'd put a card table out on the field and hit a wedge shot so it would wind up under the table. I could hit ninety-six different shots with a standard set of golf clubs."

As Mike traveled across the country putting on trick shot exhibitions, he also challenged anyone to try to outdrive him for a five-thousand-dollar prize. Mike never lost a long-drive contest, and the shows and side bets earned him a fortune. "I lived like a maharaja," he said. "I drove everywhere in a Cord, the best car you could drive back then. And everywhere I went people were waiting to watch me play."

In 1939, Mike was offered a job at the Wilshire Country Club in Beverly Hills, California. He never did take the job, but the offer drew him to the West Coast, where he began a whole new chapter of his life.

"I'll have to stop you there, Mike," I said picking up the check and signaling for the waitress to take my credit card. "Before we go any further, I need to make sure you have a chance to look at my swing. The article I'm writing for the *Times* will be focusing on the swing you developed and your ability as a teacher, so I need to get a lesson from you."

Graziella approached our table cautiously, her dark eyes revealing a wariness of Mike. He spoke to her in Italian and again she blushed. Watching the interplay between this desirable woman and this once-handsome, still-dangerous man, I knew I was viewing a world I had never been a part of. And what I felt once again stirred those confusing feelings about Mike that both attracted and repelled me. But more than anything, it showed me that, all too often, a writer is only a witness, a spectator. I would never be a full participant in the passionate arenas of life that Mike had known.

CHAPTER 5

A HANDS-ON LESSON

Mike, Dr. Tom, and I drove back to Mike's house on Irondale Avenue and pulled up in front of the one-story bungalow on the corner of the block. We decided to go inside and talk for a few minutes about the swing in general before I had my first hands-on lesson. I knew Mike would apply the term "hands-on teaching" to me very literally. As we walked across the parched lawn, under the blazing afternoon sun, I saw the golf mat, with the groove worn down the center, and the aluminum lawn chair that Mike sat in while teaching. My stomach tightened as I realized I would soon be the focus of Mike's harsh scrutiny.

While still inside Mike's house, I paused to look at the sequence shots of famous golfers' swings, the trophies and clubs lying around the room. Behind Mike's Barcalounger, a sliding glass door opened onto a patio that was completely filled with golf equipment. There were sets of irons, drivers, and boxes filled with the Flammer. I had the urge to go out and search among the boxes to see what treasures and oddities I could find. For a moment, I wondered if the club he had set the *Guinness* record with would be there. Then I remembered it was in the World Golf Hall of Fame in Florida.

Dr. Tom, who had been listening to all this golf talk very patiently, took a seat on the sofa in the corner, while Mike settled in the hulking Barcalounger. I noticed a strange-looking golf club tucked into the cushions of the chair. It was only about a foot and a half long—not much more than just a grip and the clubhead.

"What's that for?" I said, pointing to this shortened club.

"To demonstrate the correct action of the hands," he said, picking it up. "Come here, I'll show you."

I moved over and stood in front of his chair.

"If you grip the club this way and take it back, it's easier to watch what the clubhead is doing. What I teach my students is how to keep the club on line, true to all the points in the compass, throughout the swing. Understand?"

I nodded, watching his ancient hands slowly rotating the club in a half circle.

"What the pros don't understand is that at the top of their swing their wrists are uncocked, like this. See?" I leaned over for a better look.

"Now, this is how my wrists are at the top of my swing." He bent his wrist in the opposite direction as if ready to give someone a backhanded slap.

I bent over him, fascinated. Maybe my lack of power was due to this very reason.

"See how powerful this is?" There was a menacing tone in

Mike's voice that caused me to shift my eyes to his. He was staring at me with focused intensity as he growled, "Hell, I could break your goddamned scapula with this action. Just like this, *BAM!*" He flicked his hand but stopped just short of my collarbone.

I forced myself to hold my ground despite the fact that I felt he really might try to strike me, just to make his point.

"This is where you generate power for the release?" I asked, straightening slowly, out of range now. "This is the supple quickness you've said is the basis of distance?"

"Hell, yes. Hold out your *hund,* I want to show you something," he said in a rumbling voice, his accent hinting at both Scotland and the Deep South.

I obeyed. He smacked the palm of my hand with the flat of the backside of his left hand while holding his wrist straight.

"Did that hurt?" he asked.

"Not really."

"Now, this is accelerating." He cocked his wrist and flicked it as he hit my hand with a loud, crisp *smack*. Later, listening to my tape recording of this interview, I was amazed at the difference in the pitch between these two blows. I nodded, impressed, then sat in a chair nearby, my hand stinging.

"You release the contraction of the muscles, and it becomes a free-moving object," Mike said. "You are actually freezing muscle if you flex it. If you do that you slow down your swing."

"Mike," I said, rubbing my hand, "how would you describe your swing as compared to the swing that's taught by PGA pros?"

"The PGA?" he scoffed. "Hell, the PGA wouldn't piss on me if my guts were on fire. Most of the tour professionals need pros to teach them."

"All right. Just take me through your swing. How would you describe it?"

He suddenly calmed down and said, "There are six types of joints, and they have to work according to their design. My swing conforms to the basic laws of physics. All the joints are working according to their design. That's called the physiology of the body. Understand?"

"Okay, but now specifically, what do you do?"

"You were asking about the tour players," Mike said, his voice growing bitter again. "Hell, those guys swing over, down, and across. With my swing I go under, up, and out."

I didn't fully understand his words, but I felt there was something profound in them. Was it really that different and that simple? For a moment, I forgot my fear of Mike's explosive temper. I even forgot my throbbing hand.

"You're saying they throw the club out at the top?"

"I'm saying my swing is more efficient and more accurate. I bend my left leg and my weight shifts back. My hips tilt up and then they turn." He augmented his words with a subtle rocking motion of his hand. "Then my hips swing back and then turn toward the target. Belly button facing the target. Understand?

66

One hip turns up, and the other turns down. My hips and shoulders do the same thing. You are shortening everything on the left side to make the backswing. This is the key, the formula, you understand? What I do is swing the meat, not the metal. The result of all this is fast hands."

"So you don't feel like you are swinging hard?"

He shook his head and stared at me, challengingly. I pondered this and glanced over to see that Dr. Tom was watching us intently. I recalled how, while shooting free throws, Tom used the mental image of a long arm dropping the ball in a basket to make the task seem simple. It made me wonder if Mike ever did something similar.

"Sometimes it helps if you have a mental picture of certain actions in sports," I asked. "Was there anything you pictured as you were hitting the ball?"

Mike replied without hesitation; there didn't seem to be anything I could ask that stumped him.

"I used to think of where I was going."

"Where you're going?"

"I saw myself standing on a map. I'm going to New York and the ball is in Kansas City. I'd just think about taking the club back to Los Angeles and go to New York going through Kansas City on the way. It gave me the arc instead of a line."

It was poetic, effective, and, of course, larger than life. I pictured a Mike Austin so large he could stand on the United States and swing across the whole country. Some people dreamed little dreams. Mike Austin saw himself as a giant, striding across the landscape.

My mind felt overheated with talk—talk about something that actually didn't exist in language but lived in the real world, beyond words. This was golf, after all, the process of hitting a small ball a long way with accuracy and control. There was only one way to learn how to achieve those abilities, to translate the words into feelings, sensations, and, ultimately, reflex. It was time for my lesson. Mike hoisted himself from his chair, and we moved outside into the white heat of the afternoon.

"Doctor," Mike said to Dr. Tom. "Get an extra chair and sit in the shade there. It's hotter than hell out here. Phil, put the mat there . . ." I picked up the mat and positioned it near Mike's chair. "Not there," he said impatiently. "There! Don't you see? There! Facing that way!"

I adjusted the mat and then, under Mike's direction, began to set up a device that dangled a ball from a rope. When you hit the ball it spun around a short arm. The direction of the circular motion showed if you had hit a slice or a hook. Mike then wrestled an ancient video camera into position on a tripod. Watching Mike poke and pry the camera with his one good hand, cursing all the time, I realized how badly I must want to learn a better golf swing to put up with this humiliation. For some reason, the camera couldn't be coaxed into life, so at least I was saved the embarrassment of later watching myself being lambasted as I took my lesson.

Mike abandoned the idea of videotaping the lesson, saying, "We'll do the best we can without it. Go ahead and address the ball."

I had studied Mike's teaching videotape carefully, so I set up to the ball using the method he taught. Unlike other golf instructors, who tell their students to get in a semi-crouched position, Mike advocates bending forward from the ball-and-socket joints of the hips, with only a slight flex in the knees. He used to place a club along the center of his chest as he bent forward to show how the torso stays straight. In the crouched position the back tends to collapse, placing strain on the lower vertebrae of the spine.

"Good, good . . ." Mike said, watching my movements like a hawk.

I was careful to take the strong grip that Mike teaches, and as I put my right hand on the club, I let my right knee bend in a bit. My body was in a "K" position favored by big hitters. My left side was straight, and my right arm and leg angled in so I could place my hand on the golf grip.

"Now slowly make your backswing," Mike said.

Starting with a slight forward press—pushing my hands and right knee forward less than an inch—I then began to draw the club back. And that's when it started.

"No, sir!" Mike's voice shattered the still air like a sonic boom. "Don't roll the left wrist over! You'll lose all your power."

I tried to interpret his instruction so I could rectify my motion.

"Not that way!" Mike was aghast at what he saw, his voice filled with pain, horrified to see a student of his in the wrong position. "Look. Can you even do this?" He held out his left arm and rotated the hand in the opposite direction. "It goes under, not over. Under! NO! Not like that! Like this!"

Once more I took my position. And once more I remembered all those torturous incidents from school, standing at the blackboard, chalk in hand, my math teacher waiting for me to solve a problem as the entire class looked on, snickering. I felt the same way now. I noticed that Dr. Tom graciously had averted his eyes, not wanting to add to my humiliation.

"Okay, Mike, I'll go slowly and you tell me when I go off track." I looked over at him, his old face reddening in anger, his eyes scorching me. I began with the forward press but then started turning my wrist the opposite way. It felt very unnatural, like swimming upstream, like violating some law of nature.

"Better . . ." he said, still ready to pounce. "Now take it back farther . . . Farther . . . No, sir! At the top of the swing, the wrist is above the *hands*. Above! Jesus Christ, do you know what that means? Okay, at least see if you can do this. Go only halfway into the backswing."

Through an act of will I blocked out the anger in Mike's voice and tried to listen to his words. "Okay, halfway back."

I pulled the club back halfway according to his instructions. The position I put my wrist in felt very unnatural. Still, I sensed that I was in a position of coiled power.

"Now swing from there."

I swung and hit the ball. It spun in a true circle, showing that the ball would have flown straight.

"Work on that for now," Mike said. "When you come back, we'll take you all the way to the top. But remember, don't turn the *hands* over. Halfway through the swing you have to read the Bible."

"Do what?" I asked.

"Read the Bible. You know," he held his left hand with the palm facing him. "You know, like you're holding the Bible and reading it. Use that image, and it will keep you from turning the wrist over. All right. That's enough for now. It's too hot out here. We'll be burned to a crisp."

Later that day, driving home, I was thinking of my lesson, when Dr. Tom said, "You're doing it."

"Doing what?"

"That thing with your left hand. The thing Mike was yelling at you about."

I looked down and saw that while I gripped the steering wheel with my right hand, my free left hand was unconsciously practicing the motion Mike had recommended, as if giving someone a backhanded slap.

"Do you think that really makes a difference?" I asked Tom, still making the motion with my hand.

"How the hell should I know? I don't play golf." Then Tom started chuckling. "I thought I was going to have to come to your rescue there for a second."

Mike gives a hands-on lesson.

"Yeah. It's a good thing Mike can't really stand up easily anymore. All he can do is shout at me—which is bad enough."

"It's a hell of a way to learn," Tom said. "But he knows what he's talking about."

"You think so?"

Tom nodded. "You don't hit a ball that much farther than everyone else by accident."

It was one of the most positive things Dr. Tom had said about Mike. His words carried a lot of weight, and I was very pleased to have his endorsement of Mike's abilities.

"One thing you have to understand," Dr. Tom added. "When someone has had a stroke, it can really change their personality. What I'm saying is, if they used to smile a lot before the stroke, afterward they might grimace or frown all the time. The stroke rewires people. So maybe Mike wasn't always like this. Maybe he's frustrated by not having all his faculties."

These words from Dr. Tom stuck with me and later came to haunt me as I searched for Mike's true personality. I often wondered what Mike had been like in his pre-stroke days and always paid most attention to the descriptions of Mike from people who had known him when he was younger.

When I got home I experimented with the new position by hitting balls into a net in my backyard. When I hit a good one I could feel solid contact. But I couldn't see how far the balls were going or if they were slicing or hooking. About fifteen minutes before the sun set, however, I took my 7-iron and walked down to the golf course, which was less than a block from my house.

The seventh hole is a par-4, 428 yards, dogleg right. I checked to make sure the last group of golfers had passed and then stepped out onto the fairway at the 150-yard marker. I took five balls out of my pocket and threw them down on the grass. I took my address position and rehearsed the takeaway several times. Then I swung. The ball *clacked* off the club and went shooting forward about a foot off the ground. *What do you expect when you radically change your swing?* I thought. I raked the second ball over and hit it with much the same result. The third ball felt a little better, climbing into a steep arch and then falling short of the green. The fourth hit felt pure. And the fifth was heaven.

By now it was twilight, with only a faint memory of blue left in the darkening sky. I squinted to see where the last two balls had ended up. I saw only one white dot on the green. Oh, well. It was my first time with the new swing. But as I continued walking I didn't see the ball lying anywhere nearby. Had I hit it that badly? It felt almost perfect. Well, there was always the chance it was in the cup. I approached the flag, noticing that there was a ball mark about a foot in front of the pin. I bent to look into the hole . . . and saw the round white glow of the ball looking back up at me.

Chapter 6

The Hollywood Years

"Here's a picture that MGM studios took of me for a film test," Mike said, handing me a photo that was taken of him in 1939. "They were going to do a movie about a boxer, but they eventually scrapped it."

The black-and-white photo showed a young, muscular Mike Austin wearing only swimming trunks and posing with his fists up, ready to fight. His expression was equally fierce, but it also showed that he had striking good looks, piercing eyes, and, despite a real career as a boxer, an angular nose. Another photo he showed me from that year was taken of him at the Los Angeles Open at Riviera Country Club. He looked lean and elegant in his golf clothes, finishing a shot with his hands high, back arched.

Through the studios Mike met Errol Flynn, and the two eventually moved into an apartment in Hollywood. Mike would go to a dance hall and pick out the two most gorgeous women there. He would then go up to them and say, "How would you like to meet Errol Flynn?" Usually, they would say, "We'd do

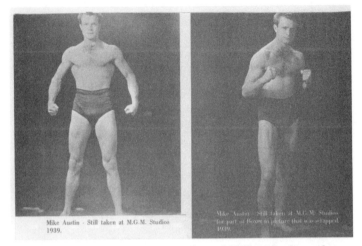

Mike Austin · Still taken at M.G.M. Studios 1939.

Mike Austin · Still taken at M.G.M. Studios for part of Boxer in picture that was scrapped. 1939.

In 1939 Mike was given a screen test for an MGM movie about a boxer. The film was never made.

anything to meet him." This was exactly what Mike wanted to hear. He told them, "Well, tonight you're going to meet him." He would take them back to his apartment and introduce the women to the heartthrob. After they had their way with the women, Mike and Errol argued about who would have to drive them home. Mike didn't really like talking about this period in his life, and all he wanted to say about the swashbuckling Flynn was that he had been "a mean drunk."

We were back at Mike's house with the tape recorder rolling, collecting more notes for the *Times* article. I sat in a straight-backed chair beside the Barcalounger, while the air conditioner struggled to keep the temperature down. Still, the heat pressed in on the small house, seeping into the room and making it stuffy.

"What was it that brought you out to Los Angeles?" I asked him.

"I played a round of golf with Bobby Jones, and he brought along a pro from one of the country clubs in Los Angeles," Mike said.

"*The* Bobby Jones?" I asked, recalling Mike's earlier association with the great champion.

"Right. When this pro saw that I could reach par-fives in two, *with a short iron,* he said to Bobby Jones, 'Where the hell did you find this guy?' Jones said, 'He's from right here in Atlanta.' 'Well,' the pro said. 'I'm taking him back to Los Angeles. He'll be the new pro at Wilshire Country Club.' But when I got out to California, I found that they had a new law, that you had to live in the state for a year before you could get a job here."

"What year was that?"

"It was nineteen thirty-nine. And they had all these Oakies coming into the state. So that's why they made the rule—to try to stop people from coming out here. So while I was waiting to take the Wilshire job, the actor who played Charlie Chan, Sidney Toler, came to me and asked me to run his driving range that was right next to Hillcrest Country Club. One day I was playing at Hillcrest, and I drove the first green, which was a downhill three-hundred-fifty-seven-yard par-four."

"Wait a second. You drove a green that was three-hundred fifty-seven yards?"

Mike nodded, his eyes holding mine steadily. "There was a guy on the green, his name was Skank—or Shank, or something like that—he was head of Fox Studios at the time. He paid me ten thousand dollars to come to a tournament that weekend and put on an exhibition. I hit fifty golf balls on that hole, and I put forty-seven of them on the green."

"You put forty-seven of fifty balls on a green that was three-hundred fifty-seven yards away?"

Mike nodded. He waited for me to challenge him. I filed the information, hoping to someday verify it. But how? Most of the information available today on the Internet began in the 1980s, when computers were first being used to collect and store news stories. Finding newspaper clippings from the decades prior to that is a huge undertaking.

"One of the people watching that event worked for the biggest talent agency in town at that time. He said, 'Come on by my office and I'll sign you to a contract for the motion pictures.' That's how I got a ten-year contract with MGM."

Sometime later, Mike showed me a book of photographs and poetry he had written. The book included his screen-test photos for MGM. In many of the pictures he was dressed in a tuxedo with tails and a top hat. This was verification of some kind. But still, I found myself always seeking to independently corroborate the things Mike said. It was intriguing to think that

Mike sang in shows such as the 1946 Los Angeles Civic Opera's Sally.

out there somewhere, in some scrapbook, were yellowing newspaper clippings of this Hillcrest exhibition. After all, forty-seven out of fifty balls on a green that was 357 yards away? That was incredible.

"Who else did you know during this time? Any other stars?" I had to ask.

"Hell, yes, I knew them all. I gave golf lessons to Bob Hope's wife . . . I played a round with Nixon. I even met——" he stopped himself.

"Yes?" I prompted him.

"How much tape do you have?"

"Plenty."

"All right," he said, taking a deep breath and sitting up straighter in his chair. "I had a driving range down near Culver

City, you see. And one afternoon in the winter, it was getting foggy, so I thought I'd close early. But I saw this cab come up and a tall man stepped out and came into the shop.

" 'I'm looking for Mike Austin,' he said.

" 'That's me, sir.'

" 'I hear you're a pretty good teacher. I need a lesson.' And he handed me a hundred-dollar bill. Well, at that time a hundred dollars was a hell of a lot of money. I said, 'I'll be happy to teach you. But why don't you let your cab go? I'll drive you anywhere you want to go afterward.' He just waved this off, so I gathered that he must be wealthy, even though he didn't dress like it. He had tennis shoes with holes in them, understand?

"I gave him a lesson, and at the end of it he gave me another hundred-dollar bill and said he wanted another lesson the next week. He came three times for lessons. Then he came again and I saw that he didn't have his clubs with him, so I realized he didn't want a lesson. He just said, 'I want you to go someplace with me.' We both got into a cab and began heading up toward Hollywood. Along the way he says to me, 'You've helped me accomplish something very important today. You see, I've been playing in a foursome for the past year. And no matter how the teams were formed, I would always lose. Over the year, I lost quite a bit of money. And I began to realize that these men, who pretended to be my friends, were conspiring against me.

" 'Today, I played against the three of them. My shot against the best ball from the three. I beat them all, and I took back all of the money I had lost. When we were done, I said, 'I know what you've been doing to me. And I want you to know that I'll have nothing more to do with you. If I see you on the street, I won't recognize you or speak to you. I will do my best to forget that I've ever known you. You have nothing more to do with my life.'

"We arrived at an address in Beverly Hills by now and I saw that it was Tavio's—the best tailor in Los Angeles. He made suits for all the stars. We went in together and this man said to the tailor, 'I want you to make Mr. Austin the finest suit that you've ever made. I want you to use the best cloth and to spare no expense in any way.' And the tailor said, 'Yes, sir, Mr. Hughes. I'll do as you ask.' "

I had been completely involved in the story, picturing it as he spoke in his rich, rumbling voice, and I now realized it was over—left to my imagination to fill in the blank. Then, of course, it hit me.

"Howard Hughes."

Mike nodded.

We sat there for a moment in silence, the air conditioner ticking away and the pictures on the walls around us were suddenly so alive it was as if I could hear them talking, as if the happy moments were not frozen any longer but playing on and on through eternity. I realized I had, at least for this moment, joined Mike's world. It was the best of two worlds because it was the past, viewed from the present, when

Howard Hughes was not one of many famous people of long ago, but a true icon.

With these thoughts, a haunting question returned to me. It was the question that would ask itself repeatedly while I wrote this book: How could Mike know so many giants from the past without winding up in the history books himself (except the *Guinness Book of World Records*)?

I thought of another icon, but this one from a different universe—Ben Hogan, "Bantam Ben" or, another nickname I actually preferred, "The Hawk," as he was called for his amazing powers of concentration.

"What about Hogan?" I asked. "Did you ever play with the Hawk?"

"Many times."

"Was he a little guy?" I had to ask it, and I expected one of Mike's pejorative responses.

"Not really," Mike said, and I thought I detected an uncharacteristic note of awe in his voice. "When you saw him in the locker room, with his shirt off, you could tell he was an athlete. He had very defined pecs and abs."

"So what was it like to play with him?"

"He never looked at you, he never talked, he never looked at his scorecard. He just smoked and played. I almost felt like he didn't know I existed. But then one night he called me."

"What did he want?"

"This was right after he got out of the hospital. He'd been in that car wreck where they thought he'd never walk again. He called me up and said he wanted to play a round at Bel Air Country Club. When we got there he told me he had had a dream about a Scotsman named Braum. 'He sliced everything,' Hogan said. 'But he hit every fairway and every green. And he finished with even par.'

"During the round, I saw that Hogan had developed a new swing. He couldn't do the same leg action, because his knees were all torn up. So he didn't shift—it was almost like a chip shot. But just like Braum, he hit every fairway and every green. And at the end of the round, he was like a kid on Christmas Day with a house full of presents."

"I heard that Hogan hooked the ball."

"He did that before the accident. He'd hit it one hundred yards out of bounds on the right so the ball could finish on the left edge of the fairway. And he hit the ball a hell of a long way. But after the accident he always faded the ball."

"Yeah, but he won a lot of tournaments."

Mike acted as if he hadn't heard me. I heard him mutter, "Very short hitter."

I glanced at my list of questions and saw I had over-looked an important area that I wanted to touch on in my article: his teaching. After all, he had those awards on his wall from the Southern California Golf Association and *Golf Digest.*

"Who would you say was your best student? Was it Mike

In the 1960s Mike taught golf, tennis, baseball,
and boxing at his school in Hollywood.

Dunaway?" I had read that name in other articles about him.
And Mike had made a more recent video with Dunaway called
Mike Austin: Secrets from the Game's Longest Hitter.

Mike thought about it. Then his expression changed and he
started chuckling.

"What's so funny?"

"Dunaway is very religious, understand? When I was

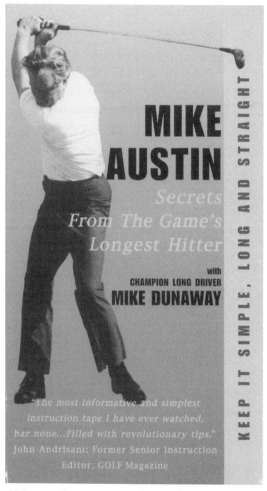

Mike teamed up with his student, Mike Dunaway, for this 1998 video.

teaching him—well, you know how I cuss—he couldn't stand to hear that. It drove him crazy."

"I'll be calling Mike Dunaway, but I wanted to hear it from you first—how did you meet him?"

"He drove up to my driving range."

"In Culver City?"

"This was much later. It was in Burbank then. He pulled up in this old VW Bug. He said to me, 'I want you to teach me to be the long-drive champion of the world.' I said, 'I can give you lessons, but it will be very expensive. How much money do you have?' He said to me, 'I don't have a dime to buy a cup of coffee. But I want you to teach me to be the world's long-drive champion.'

"I talked with him a little, and I found out he had driven all the way from Arkansas to see me. He had a football scholarship, but he tore up his knee and couldn't play anymore. And he lost his scholarship. So I said to him, 'I can't promise anything, but I'll take a look at your swing.' Well, if you had taken four driving ranges and put them side to side, he still wouldn't have kept the ball on the range, he was that wild. So here is this kid with raw power but no control at all. So I called a friend and said I need to borrow some money for a student of mine. We got a loan for eighteen thousand dollars. I worked with him all day every day, and within six months Dunaway had won the U.S. Long-Drive Championship and paid back all the money he borrowed. In nineteen-ninety he won the World Super-Long-Drive contest in Japan."

Mike started laughing again, bouncing up and down in his seat. "But, Christ, how he hated to hear me swear."

Before filing my story with the *Times*, I had a chance to call Dunaway and talk to him directly. He wasn't at all what I had expected. I imagined a serious religious person who was cautious and quiet. He was indeed thoughtful and serious much of the time, but then he would suddenly make a bold statement and follow it with a whoop of laughter. In his Arkansas twang, he said he remembered his initial meeting with Mike somewhat differently. However, he described his lessons with Mike by saying, "We darn near came to blows a couple of times. But after a while, I started videotaping all my lessons. That way, out of the heat of the moment, I could go back and see what Mike was saying." He grew serious again and added, "Mike made me what I am today. I don't have an original thought when it comes to the golf swing. Everything I know I learned from Mike."

I asked what it was like to see Mike Austin hit the ball.

"It was like you couldn't believe what you were seeing. It never looked like he was swinging hard, but he was getting it out there. Even in his seventies he was getting it way out there."

"So what was Mike's secret? What made him so long?"

Dunaway pondered the question carefully.

"He combines all the pieces of the swing better than anyone, ever. I'm telling you, when you fully grasp what Mike is teaching . . ." he groped for words. "You almost feel guilty hitting the ball so far, because it's so dang easy," he said and went off into gales of laughter again.

I called a number of other people and asked them to comment on the Mike Austin swing. Fitness guru Jack La Lanne said he took up golf at the age of fifty and, with Mike's help, became a four-handicapper. I also consulted with the experts at Farnes Golf, in Tacoma, Washington, a cutting-edge clinic where computers are used to create a 3-D picture of golfers' swings. Jon Mortensen, director of biomechanics, verified Mike's claims about the golf swing and the elements that produce distance. And finally, I placed a call to Danny Shauger, who I had heard was teaching the Austin method at one of the four golf courses in Griffith Park in Los Angeles.

"Mike Austin is a genius," Shauger told me. "But you almost have to be a genius to understand what he's saying."

This hit home with me, since Mike often told me things I sensed held great wisdom but that I didn't fully understand. At that moment I made a mental note to get golf lessons from Shauger. Maybe it would help to learn the Austin method from an additional source.

When I finally met Shauger some time later, I found he was a tall man, in his early sixties, with sandy brown hair that was thinning slightly and faded tattoos on both arms. He was a no-nonsense working-class kind of guy who spoke with a slight

New Jersey accent. He had made a living as a carpenter, building sets for the studios. While he never graduated from high school, he was well-spoken and had a great sense of humor. He was a patient teacher, who used analogies to quickly convey sequences of motions in one apt comparison.

On the phone that day Shauger told me another thing that really struck me. "I never had a close relationship with my father," he said. "Basically, I grew up on the streets and got in a lot of trouble. Mike was a father figure to me. He straightened me out. He taught me his golf swing and I've made a living teaching it. I have to say, I really love the man."

Love. That was a word I hadn't heard in connection with Mike Austin. His world didn't seem to have much room in it for love. He was a product of an earlier generation, a generation even before my own parents, whose personalities were forged during the Depression. Mike came from a time when it was important to be the biggest, the strongest, and the most powerful. He never lost the need to prove himself by beating the men around him, winning their money or exceeding their accomplishments. But now Shauger was introducing this word *love.* And it took me completely by surprise. But when I thought of it, I realized how well it fit their relationship. Mike didn't have any children. And Danny Shauger was never close to his father. They had come together on the golf course and filled a void in each other's lives. Thinking of this made Mike human to me for the first time.

I took all these notes and wove them into my *Times* article. Although I had only begun to scratch the surface about what made Mike Austin's swing so superior to the commonly taught swing, there seemed to be three primary differences. First, Mike transferred his weight by tilting his hips rather than turning them. Second, he fully released the head of the club with a throwing motion that began at the top of his swing, not in a delayed fashion, as taught by most instructors. And finally, Mike claimed that his swing used the joints of the body in the way they were designed. This avoided the twisting motion that led to chronic back and joint injuries.

I felt I understood the Austin swing in theory. But I hadn't been able to put it into practice yet. I often thought of what Dunaway had said about Austin's swing being so easy: "You almost felt guilty hitting it so far." Well, I wasn't hitting it far and I wasn't feeling the least bit guilty. But I really, really wanted to feel the guilt. My swing had improved a lot, but I was far from my goal of hitting a 300-yard drive. Still, every time I went to see Mike it reignited my feeling that a good swing, the magic swing, was within my reach. But as the deadline for my *Times* article approached, I had few tangible results to report. I stepped up my practicing and consulted Mike's teaching videotapes often.

I've noticed that with golf you never know when lightning is going to strike—you never know when you will make a giant leap forward in your ability. That's why I keep coming back to the game and struggling through rounds of golf where I hack my way around the course. I feel this undying urge to get it right, to strike the ball crisply every time, to play the game the way it was meant to be played.

Just before my *Times* deadline, I drove down to San Diego to play a round of golf with a friend of mine named Phil Lebherz. The starter put us in with a stocky, powerful guy who told us he had been a U.S. Navy SEAL. The three of us teed off at dawn and reached the sixth hole, a 143-yard par-3, an hour later. I teed up the ball and put a Mike Austin swing on it. I looked up to see I had hit a nice high draw that began working its way back toward the pin.

"It's looking good," Phil said. "It's looking really good . . ."

"It's right on the pin," the ex-Navy SEAL said.

Then, *wham*, the ball struck the flagstick and ricocheted to a distant corner of the green. When we walked up to the green, I found my ball mark six inches from the hole. It had caromed off the stick and nearly slam-dunked into the hole—then come to rest 30 feet from the hole. This certainly confirmed Mike's claim of teaching a swing that provided pinpoint accuracy.

Later in the round, I verified another of Mike's claims. I hit a drive that took off on a good arc and then hung there in the air. It had that solid feeling that comes up through the shaft, into your arms and shoulders, and seems to make your entire body warm with satisfaction.

"Your swing was different that time," Phil said. "You got more ass into it."

When I reached the ball, it was 260 yards down the center of the fairway. More importantly, it was 20 yards in front of my playing partners, and they were both brawny guys. I thought of what Mike had told me in the beginning: "Distance has little to do with size or strength. Distance comes from supple quickness."

I recorded these results in my article and filed it with my editor at the *Times*. The story bounced back and forth for many rewrites and then was placed in a cue of articles waiting to be published. It languished there for a month or more, and each week would bring a call from Mike asking when it would run. He invited me up to his house for more lessons, but time and distance—he lived forty-six miles away from me on the other side of the Los Angeles area—didn't allow it.

Finally, I got an email from the *Times* saying the story would run on October 7, 2001. There was even talk of making it the cover story that Sunday. But Mike was eventually replaced by a cover story about the use of crystal methamphetamine in the gay community.

I called Mike to tell him to watch for the story that weekend and added, as I always do, that stories are often postponed. Things can change at any moment, I said. But the article finally appeared along with a picture of Mike, his white eyebrows curled up at the edges, holding a golf ball out toward the camera, under the headline: THE MAN WHO CRACKED THE CODE.

Reviewing a preview copy of the story, I felt a spark of satisfaction knowing that I had brought some recognition to a man whose amazing accomplishments never really got the attention they deserved.

CHAPTER 7

IN THE LIMELIGHT

On the Sunday when the profile of Mike ran in the *Times,* my phone rang early in the morning. I had a hunch who might be calling and I braced myself.

"Phil? Mike Austin," he sounded almost breathless. "Listen, buddy, you did one *hell* of a job with this write-up. It's the best damn piece I've ever read."

"I had good material to work with, Mike," I said. I was relieved, because you never know how people will react when they read a profile of themselves.

"I'm telling you, the damn phone has been ringing off the hook," he chuckled. "I'm selling Flammers hand over fist." A picture flashed into my mind of Mike, sitting in his Barcalounger with a big grin on his face.

I heard an interruption on the line, meaning that he had another call coming in. "Here's another call. I have to go. But I want you to come up to the house. I have a present for you."

"Sounds great, Mike. Enjoy your day. You deserve this."

"You are a great writer, buddy," he said, then hung up.

That Sunday I often pictured Mike fielding calls from long-drive hopefuls like myself, taking orders for the Flammer and booking lessons. But the next day my good mood came to an abrupt end. My friend Martin Smith, the editor for the Mike Austin article, called me.

"We have a problem," Marty said. "We've gotten a bunch of calls about your story. Most people just want to know where they can get that Flammer thing. But this one woman worries me."

"Why?"

"She knows Mike Austin, and she claims he is a fraud."

Fraud. The word went deep into my heart. And as it did, I realized I had never completely banished my own feelings of doubt about Mike and his accomplishments. Maybe he really was a fraud and I had been played for a sucker. I couldn't help but think of the millions of copies of the Sunday *Times Magazine* with a glaring error in it. It was the worst feeling a journalist can have.

"She's saying that Mike never hit the long drive?"

"No, no. Not that. She said he doesn't have these degrees you list in the story—physics, engineering, and a PhD in kinesiology. Damn, I wish we had just attributed it to him, then we'd be off the hook. But we've got it in here as a fact. So you better check it out. We'll print a retraction if we have to. But I really hope we don't have to."

Marty gave me the woman's name and a telephone number in the Los Angeles area.

Before I could call her, my phone rang. It was my friend

Louis Lebherz, brother of Phil, with whom I had golfed in San Diego. Lou was a basso profundo in the Los Angeles Opera Company and we often played golf together. At six feet, six inches tall and weighing in at 320 pounds, Lou definitely had the size and strength to become the longest hitter around. But he was frustrated by a slice he couldn't seem to cure.

"You won't believe what happened at the opera last night," he said, his voice rich and deep, even over the phone line.

My mind was still on this woman, Irene, who had called the *Times*, so I mumbled, "What happened?"

"I got a visit in my dressing room from a mysterious stranger. Do you remember Ricky Leech, the tenor we've golfed with a couple of times?"

"Yeah."

"I played with him last week and he was hitting the crap out of the ball. I asked him what he had done, and he said he was taking lessons from a guy named Danny Shauger up at Griffith Park."

"I talked to him for the *Times* article."

"Wait a second," Lou said. "You're gonna love this. So I'd just finished doing *La Traviata*, and I'm taking off my makeup when Ricky Leech comes in and says he's got someone he wants me to meet. In walks—"

"Mike Austin."

"Yes! It was the most amazing thing. This Danny Shauger was one of Mike's students. So listen, Mike looked me over and got this big grin on his face. He said, 'You're a giant of a man!' Then I told him I'd seen your story about him that day in the *Times*, so I asked him for a lesson sometime. Next thing I know, he's got me and Leech out in the hallway and he's knocking us all over the place. He's showing me how to flex my left knee and all of a sudden he shouts: '*No, sir!*' and whacks my knee with his cane."

Lou's laughter boomed through the telephone. I could picture the whole scene, Mike taking control of the two men, giving them lessons in the hallway while they still had on wigs and makeup. I wished I could fully enjoy it, but I still had this woman's call hanging over my head.

"I'm in a real bind over that article," I said. "I've got this woman calling the *Times* and telling them Mike's a fraud."

"Why?"

"She saying there's no way he has all these degrees he claims he has."

"She's probably right."

"What?" This wasn't what I needed.

"When I read that in your story it didn't ring true."

"Why not?"

"My sister has a degree in kinesiology, and they just created the program about twenty years ago. It was brand-new then."

"The worst part is I've always been a little suspicious myself," I said. "But I couldn't verify his claims, because they were from so long ago."

"He's still an entertaining guy. Let's go up and see him sometime. I want a lesson."

I hung up and dialed the woman's number. As the phone rang, I could hear my own breath in the receiver, quick and shallow. A woman answered and I identified myself. Irene had an intelligent, classy voice, and she sounded like she was probably in her sixties.

"I understand you know Mike Austin," I said, easing into the subject in a neutral way.

"I've known him and his wife for probably thirty years. And I think there's something you should know."

"Okay."

"He's a fraud."

"Why do you say that?"

"There is no way he has those degrees that you have listed in the story."

"How do you know?"

"Mike Austin never studied anything except how to bully and intimidate people."

"I'm sorry, I don't follow you."

"Many times I'd been at dinners and heard him go on about how he had degrees in this or that. And if anyone said one word that contradicted Mike, he would become furious."

"I know he has a temper. But that doesn't make him a fraud."

"But you know he is."

99

Her comment startled me. Because in a way it was what I'd been feeling.

"Did you call these colleges that are listed here?" she asked.

"No," I said. "I had no reason to doubt him. There is only so far we can go in fact checking."

"Call them. You'll see he's lying."

I was beginning to feel a little relief. At least she didn't have positive proof that he was a fraud. And she never challenged his golf record. The picture was beginning to come into focus. Irene didn't like Mike's manner, so she was trying to throw a shadow over his day in the sun.

"Well, I'll check into this and let you know what I find out."

"He's a fraud."

"I'll check into it."

We said good-bye and I hung up. Something seemed wrong with this story. Also, it was clear this woman had an ax to grind.

I relayed my conversation with Irene to Marty, my editor at the *Times*. He seemed somewhat relieved. Still, he added, "You better run all this past Iron Mike, see what his response is. If you're satisfied, then we'll let it stand. But we have to follow up a little more."

I sat on my feelings for the rest of the day, waiting for some clarity. Finally, I knew I couldn't keep my suspicions bottled up any longer. I dialed Mike's number. He answered immediately, his voice still excited, probably from all the attention he was getting.

"I've never seen anything like this before," Mike said. "I must have gotten three hundred phone calls. And one of them was from Sylvester Stallone. He's coming up for a lesson."

"Great," I said. Impatiently I moved on. "Look, Mike, some of the editors at the *Times* wanted me to verify a few things."

"I must have sold fifty Flammers!"

"It's concerning your academic credentials."

"My what?"

"Credentials. He wants me to make sure I got everything right." In the past, I had always been intimidated by Mike. Now, I realized, I was angry because I had been put in an embarrassing position.

"I want to run through these degrees with you. You got your engineering degree where?"

"Emory University."

"And was it a BS?"

"A what?"

"A Bachelor of Science?"

"Yes."

"And the physics degree. Where was that from?"

"Georgia Tech."

"Okay, and your doctorate in kinesiology?" I knew this would be the one that was most in doubt. "Where was that from?"

"I think they called it the National Academy of Applied Science."

You *think* they called it that? I couldn't help but be alarmed.

"What year?"

"In nineteen forty-six."

"You know, I searched on the Internet for that school and I couldn't find it. Where was it located?"

"On North Spring Street in Los Angeles."

In his voice I detected a questioning note, as if he was wondering why I was grilling him. But I couldn't stop myself. I was still mad.

"You know, I tried to find the school and there's no listing for it."

"It was a temporary campus. They set it up right after the War."

That fit. I knew the L.A. area was really growing then and college classes were held wherever space could be found for returning G.I.s.

"But if you had been in the War, how could you get a PhD the year after it was over?"

"I came back to the States in 'forty-four because I'd been in a plane wreck. My credits from medical school and psychology applied to the kinesiology degree. They didn't have an established department yet. I designed my own program and wrote a thesis."

"On what?"

"The golf swing."

I felt my anger subsiding somewhat. Besides that, Mike didn't have the defensive reaction that sometimes comes when someone is trying to hide the truth. He was very matter-of-fact, doing the best he could to answer my questions. Everything he told me was logical and plausible. Fortunately, there didn't seem to be a glaring reason to print a retraction.

KINESIOLOGY HELPS AUSTIN IN PGA WIN

BY SHAV GLICK
Times Staff Writer

"If you practice kinesiology, the science of muscle movement, you don't need to play often to play well."

It was Mike Austin, the crusty old proprietor of the Austin School Golf in downtown Hollywood, talking. And he had listeners, too, after sidelining Babe Lazane and Eddie Merrins Friday to move into today's quarterfinals of the $15,000 Southern California PGA tournament at Recreation Park.

Andreason, who admits to 51, also advanced with impressive wins over Pat Martin and Monte Sanders. Andreason, who grew up in Long Beach playing Recreation Park, holds the course record of 63—which he has done four times.

Like Austin, Andreason spends most of his time teaching. Also like Austin, he makes important use of mirrors in his "golf studio" at the Big Tee Golf Center in Buena Park. He recently left the head pro's job at Yorba Linda CC to become

Knowledge of kinesiology helped Mike redesign the golf swing.

"Okay, Mike, I just wanted to go over that since there were questions about it."

"No problem, buddy," he said. "You've got to come up to the house. I've got something for you."

"Sure. I'll call you soon."

I said good-bye and hung up. I called Marty at the *Times* and relayed the information to him. He listened carefully.

I concluded by saying, "I'll call Emory and Georgia Tech, if you want. But I don't know what to do about the National Academy of Applied Science. It's not there anymore."

"No. At this point don't worry about it. We've done enough due diligence to answer this woman's questions. Besides, the story is about his golf, and all of that is well documented. So I think we're okay."

The episode stuck in my memory for some time. When I first met Mike I assumed that his wild claims were lies. But the more I knew him, the more I realized he had a rigidly honest streak in him. Perhaps it was because he had worked as a physicist and an engineer. To produce accurate results in those fields you had to begin with precise data. What threw me off was that most people didn't have Mike's man-over-board approach to living. They took the small accomplishments and made the most of them in barroom boasting sessions. Mike's accomplishments, on the other hand, were truly herculean, so by comparison his record seemed too amazing to believe.

For a while I felt sorry that I had doubted Mike and felt bad about giving him the third degree. But another part of me was glad I had, particularly since his claims had, once again, held up under scrutiny. It made me feel that I should take a new approach with Mike: I would assume everything he said was true. After all, life was short and my time with Mike was limited. If I wanted to get the most out of our relationship, I would have to open my mind to a new world of possibilities. It was an uncomfortable feeling for me to do this. After all, I was a journalist, a professional skeptic, and this felt like I was losing control. But as I've heard it said, to discover a new land, you have to first lose sight of the shore.

CHAPTER 8

A GIANT OF A MAN

Lou Lebherz was eager to see Mike again after their brief meeting at the opera. A month later I drove up to Mike's house with Lou, who was itching to take a golf lesson. He wanted to learn to hit the long ball, of course, but more immediately, he hoped to straighten out his slice. Lou's sheer size encouraged him to try to overpower the ball. He puffed his cheeks out before starting the backswing, and then used all the force of his massive body to hit the ball. Unfortunately, the result was sometimes a banana ball that ran off the fairway and burrowed into the rough. I knew the frustration well.

I certainly hoped Lou would find the answer to his problem, but I had a hidden agenda: I wanted to watch Lou get a lesson in hopes that I could absorb the information while staying out of the line of fire. Lou's years in the opera, working with egotistical singers, taught him not to be easily intimidated. He could put up with Mike's yelling to get the swing he wanted.

I didn't tell Mike that Lou was coming, only that I was

bringing a friend who wanted to meet him. On the way, Lou said, "Do you think we should bring Mike something?"

"Like what?"

"A cake or a pie or something."

I drove in silence, thinking it over. This was new territory for me, bringing something to a friend rather than maintaining a professional distance as a journalist.

"That's a good idea. But what should we get him?" I left matters of food up to Lou since, at 320 pounds, the subject of eating was always on his mind.

"I'm thinking maybe . . ." Lou hummed a little, as if waiting for a divine message. "Lemon meringue pie."

"You think?"

"Definitely. Definitely lemon meringue pie."

We stopped at a Marie Callender's restaurant, and when I ordered the pie, the woman asked if she should cut it. I again deferred to Lou. He nodded seriously. "Oh, yes. They have a special knife and they know how to do it. We'd make a mess out of it."

The woman happily sliced the pie and put it in a box. But at the register, Lou was suddenly absent and I found myself paying for the entire thing, even though it was Lou's idea that "we" should bring something.

When we got to the little house on Irondale, we found Mike in his chair looking very sharp, indeed. His white hair was combed back, and he wore a crisp blue shirt with a buttoned collar. The house was picked up and coffee was brewing on the stove. He had put out chocolate and a dish of nuts.

"There he is!" Mike belted out cheerfully as I walked through the door and into the dimly lit interior. The TV was blasting some afternoon talk show.

"Hey, Mike," I said, talking over the TV. I took his left hand and felt the parchment-smooth skin and the cool but strong grip. Looking down at him, I saw his pale blue eyes sparkling with excitement.

"Mike, I brought someone to see you." Lou stepped out of the hallway and into the living room. He seemed to fill the entire room. I saw Mike's eyes grow wide.

"This is Lou Lebherz—I understand you met him at the opera several weeks ago."

"Why, yes, I did, Mr. Lebherz. Is it Leb-herz?"

"Herz," Lou said. "Like the hairs on top of your head. It's German. And look what we brought you." He opened the box and bent down to show it to him. A huge grin spread across Mike's face.

"My favorite. Get some plates out of the kitchen," he said to me. "Let's have a piece right now. I made coffee for you, Phil."

I got the plates, and when I returned to Mike's chair-side Lou was already singing for him. It was a piece I didn't recognize, but as he reached the lower register, the plates in my hands seemed to vibrate with the sound waves. As the piece progressed, Mike joined in singing and they finished together, holding the note and then breaking into satisfied laughter.

I served the pie, and as I handed the plate to Mike he licked his lips like a kid.

"Lemon meringue is my favorite," he said. "When I was a boy, if my mother wanted to cheer me up, she'd bake me a lemon meringue pie. Then we'd sit there in the kitchen and eat the whole damn thing."

As he spoke, I looked over to see him happily wading into the pie, bits of the fluffy white meringue flecking his lips. He looked like a big kid, and I imagined him with his mother, eating their favorite treat. But the part that kept coming back to me was that he said his mother baked the pie to cheer him up. I had never thought of Mike as suffering from bad moods— or even having moods at all. In my mind, he had the emotional range of granite. But I was beginning to see that wasn't true.

"Phil, I've got something to show you," Mike said, still eating. "Take a look at that." He waved his sticky fork over his shoulder at a new addition to his wall of photographs, awards, and plaques. I moved in for a closer look. There was the *Times* article I had written about Mike. It was mounted on a wooden background, covered with several layers of lacquer and then beautifully framed.

"That's the best damned write-up I've ever gotten," Mike said. "You are one hell of a writer. Did you read that?" he said to Lou.

"Great story," Lou said helping himself to another slice of pie.

So there I was, my name on Mike Austin's wall of fame. I was pleased to see my name included among the golfing greats of history. But an adolescent desire—completely impossible—made me wish I were there because of an athletic accomplishment, not for an egghead activity like writing. I always wanted to be doing, rather than just *thinking*. But when it came to doing things, I wasn't half the man Mike was. It reminded me of my 300-yard goal and how I was hoping to reach it by following Mike's teachings.

"I told Lou you might help him straighten out his slice," I said to Mike.

"Sure," he said, but then the hawk eye returned, spotting an effort to get something for nothing. "But I don't give lessons for free."

"No, of course not," Lou said, picking up a club that was lying nearby. "But maybe we can just talk about it in general terms. Phil tells me your swing is more powerful and more accurate than what the pros teach."

"When I was on the tour, if you were to pull any club out of my bag," Mike said, "you'd find a dime-sized smooth area worn into the metal that was exactly on the sweet spot. I never missed the sweet spot. Every shot was pure."

"That's what I want," Lou said, waggling the club. "Maybe I can get the swing right in my mind first. I understand you don't turn the hips, you tilt them." Lou took his stance and addressed an imaginary ball. "Now, when I take the club back, do I–"

"No, sir!" Mike roared. He started trying to fight his way out of the chair.

"You don't have to get up," Lou said. "I'll come closer."

He moved a foot away and Mike's hands were instantly on Lou, twisting, molding him like a sculptor.

"The hands don't turn over," Mike said. "You do that you lose all your power, because your hands are uncocked at the top of your backswing."

"Under?" Lou experimented with the motion.

"Yes, under! Not like that! Look here. Can you at least do this?" He held his left hand so the palm was facing him. "From here I've got a hell of a lot of power in my wrist."

"But, it's so different than everything I've seen before."

"It different because it uses the levers of the body the way they're supposed to be used."

"When I watch the tour players on TV they're not doing this."

"And they're not hitting the ball the way I did!" Mike bellowed. "Besides, you ever see all the copper bands the pros wear–and the magnets and the way they disappear for back surgery after a few years on the tour? My swing is based on leverage–not turning your body into a goddamned rubber band."

I had been following all this closely–at once amused by

seeing Big Lou in the hot seat, but also able to absorb details that I would otherwise have lost in the heat of the moment.

"Mike," I said, "You said something the last time I was here about how the tour players swing—out, across, and—"

"The pros teach a swing that goes over, down, and across. My swing goes under, up, and out."

There it was again, the prickling feeling of a crystallized truth. A truth I didn't yet have the ability to understand, but one that I sensed was accurate. Still, it was hard for me to believe that it was that simple. And expressed that simply. The contrast of three words: not *over, down,* and *across* but instead *under, up,* and *out.* Okay, so that was the result. But the question remained: How did you move your body to produce these results?

"So, Mike," I interrupted, "When you would swing, your club would actually cross the target line?"

"Hell, man!" he answered, his eyes still throwing thunderbolts at both of us, "My club crossed the line and my goddamned hands came all the way out to the line of flight. That's how you fully release the head of the club."

Lou got back into position. "Look, Mike, is this right?"

I could see Mike struggling to control himself. "Better. But look here. This is all you need to remember. The right arm has only three positions. On the backswing the right arm is bent and winds up in a throwing position—as if you're going to throw the football. At impact it is straight. You put back everything you've taken away—you straighten what was folded. On the follow-through the left arm folds automatically. Look here——" He folded the arm, straightened it in a downward position, then folded it again. "That's all there is to it. Combine that with the pivot and you have a golf swing."

Lou rehearsed the motion. "Like this?" He made a back-swing and held it.

"Your *hunds* are right, but you've got no power in your hips. The hips don't turn—that's what the pros these days do. They spin on their asshole. You want power, you have to *tilt* the hips."

"Show me how to do it," Lou challenged him.

"Get back in the address position," Mike growled.

Lou obeyed.

"Now bend the left leg. No, sir! Get the heel off the ground. How the hell are you going to make your turn if you don't get the heel off the ground?"

Lou returned to his address position, then bent the left knee and raised the heel so just the ball of his left foot was on the floor.

"When you do that, what happens?" Mike demanded.

"My shoulder is lowered."

"Exactly. Your left side is being shortened and you can turn around your right leg. It's like the right side of the body is a gate on a hinge."

Carefully avoiding furniture, Lou swung the club back and

arrived in a position I'd never seen him strike on the golf course. He looked coiled and powerful. I knew if he could initiate his downswing from there, and stay in control, he would knock the ball out of sight. I could almost see his drives and hear his whoops of joy. Why did I think that bringing Lou up here was a good idea?

Lou was holding the position, waiting for Mike to take him into the downswing. I saw Mike's sharp eyes scanning Lou's body. Finally, he nodded his approval.

"Now you shift your weight."

"How?" Lou croaked, straining to hold the position.

"Your right leg flexes. This lowers your right side and allows the shoulders to turn around the base of the neck like a spoke on a wheel."

Lou tried to follow the instructions.

"No, sir!" Mike bellowed. "You're swinging with your arms only. That's like tearing the spoke off a wheel. The whole machine has to move. Go back to the top and then flex the right leg—without moving anything else!"

Something clicked in my mind and the picture became complete. I stood up and grabbed club from Lou. "Let me show you," I said, taking the club to the top of the backswing. I flexed my right knee and, sure enough, if I shifted correctly, the club traveled about three feet without my arm swinging away from my chest at all. The shoulders turned like a wheel and the club dropped onto the right plane.

"Now you're coming at the ball from the inside," Mike said, sharing my enthusiasm as if he had just discovered the secret himself. "Hell, man, from there you can knock the ball farther than any son of a bitch on the golf course."

Lou copied the movements and rehearsed the shift several times. He turned to me, his face excited. "What a different feeling!"

"Yeah," I said. "You're getting your weight behind it."

"Mike," Lou said. "I can make these movements here. I understand these movements. But how do I learn this so that it becomes automatic? How can I take this out onto the course?"

"Only seven percent of what you learn comes through your ears," Mike said. "About eighty-five percent of what you learn comes through the eyes. But to really learn a physical action like the golf swing, you have to learn it through the perceptor nerve."

"I don't think I have one of those," Lou said, laughing.

"Everyone does. But the perceptor nerve doesn't have any eyes and it doesn't have any ears. You have to experience the swing through your own nervous system, through the sensations you only feel. Understand?"

"Not really."

"How about this, then," Mike said, his eyes sparkling with mischief. "If you move your ass back as much as you move your head down, the cheeks of your butt will equal the weight of your brain so you have a center of balance at your navel. You aren't swinging around your shoulders, you are swinging around your navel."

Lou had been trying to follow what Mike was saying but got lost halfway through this outrageous statement. He closed his eyes and threw his head back, and a volcano of laughter erupted from deep inside him. Mike joined in, and the two of them laughed as if they were singing another duet. I thought it was pretty funny too, but I couldn't join in. I was thinking of the swing and how to translate all this to achieve my 300-yard goal. I was in and out of my thoughts, and each time I returned to the room, the two of them were still laughing. Lou bent over Mike, pounding his shoulder, Mike's old face suddenly looking five decades younger.

" 'The cheeks of my butt equal the weight of my brain,' " Lou repeated. "That's too much, you know that?"

We got to talking about other things, and Mike told Lou some of his best stories of flying cargo planes in Africa during WWII, of winning fistfights and outdriving challengers, of loving beautiful women and debating the great minds of the world. There was a bond between the two men, even after this short meeting, that I had not experienced with Mike. I felt left out. I wondered what it was in me that always seemed to hold back. If I were simply able to let go, give everything without reserve, would I achieve the goals I was after as an athlete and a writer? And maybe then I could finally become a true companion for Mike.

Lou and I had been there for nearly three hours when I finally said it was time for us to leave.

"Before you go," Mike said to me, "I have something for you—to thank you for the article. It's right there." He pointed across the room. I followed his finger and saw two golf clubs resting in the corner—a 1-iron and a driver. These were the clubs that Mike had designed. The driver had an air foil running along the perimeter, like the fin on an old Cadillac. The 1-iron had a small head and was beautifully crafted with a tungsten rod behind the sweet spot. Along the sole of the club was the inscription "Mike Austin."

"This is beautiful, Mike," I said. "I've always wanted a driving iron."

"I used to hit that one-iron off the fairway and knock the son of a bitch two hundred and fifty yards—on the carry," Mike growled.

"I've got a great club," I said, "now I need to learn to hit it."

"You will," Mike said. "I've been watching you. You're getting it."

I was shocked. Mike had never said anything encouraging to me before. In his voice was both encouragement and pride. That was because I was his student. He was hard on his students—but he was undyingly proud of them too.

The 1-iron Mike gave me was a beautiful club, a work of art, and I wanted more than anything to develop a swing that was worthy of it. I pictured myself moving to the first tee and pulling out—not a driver, but a 1-iron—the ultimate class move. That would impress the hell out of anyone I was playing with, particularly if I hit it crisply, a sizzling shot that flew high and straight and then floated lazily to a soft landing. But what were the odds of my hitting a shot like that? At the time, I didn't hit any long irons. Instead, when I needed something below a 5-iron, I used a 7-wood. Now, with this gift, I had a new club to live up to, a new challenge from Mike. But, I realized, if I just developed a good repeatable swing, I could hit any club in the bag.

We said our good-byes, and Mike struggled out of his chair and accompanied us to the door. He was still giving instructions to Lou. Standing just outside the front door, in the chilly night air, Mike said, "Just remember this. This is the action of the right arm." Of course he was paralyzed on his right side, so he made the motion with his left arm—straight at address, bent at the top of the swing, then fully extended at impact. "That's all there is to it." Lou made the motion with his right arm, then looked to Mike for approval. Mike nodded and said nothing.

When I got back home that night, I tried hitting the 1-iron into the net in my backyard. Mike was right about one thing. When you found the sweet spot backed up by the tungsten rod, all the energy went from the head of the club into the ball. The impact was so pure it didn't even make a sound. Maybe, as Mike said, I really was making progress.

CHAPTER 9

MIKE AUSTIN VS. THE PGA

Mike Austin turned pro when he was eighteen years old, which was around 1930, the year Bobby Jones captured the Grand Slam by winning all four major golf tournaments as an amateur. I feel sure that Mike was proud to become a PGA member. In fact, he once wrote a poem called "PGA Image" in which he urged fellow professional golfers to set a good example for all golfers. Over the years, however, Mike's respect for the PGA slowly changed to disdain.

It took me a long time to understand Mike's position on both the PGA and the swing taught by PGA professionals. There is still an element of mystery surrounding this in my mind on one particular issue. In order for Mike to get his PGA card, he had to demonstrate his knowledge of the PGA-approved swing, even if he didn't agree with it. So, it seems he developed the ability to use certain PGA-sanctioned motions in his swing even though he later abandoned them.

To complicate things, Mike told me several times that he had improved his hand action about twelve years ago. Well, if you did the math this meant that he changed his hand action around the time he had his stroke. It is even possible that this "change" came after he was partially paralyzed and confined to his Barcalounger. True, he continued hitting balls with one hand (he could swat a 5-iron one-handed 150 yards on the fly). Still, it seems that he never played competitively using the hand action that he now teaches his students.

Mike's contempt for the PGA as a governing body stemmed from the episode when he discovered that the PGA's commissioner was taking bribes not to pair golfers with him. Mike hit the ball so far that other golfers looked foolish by comparison and feared they might lose their sponsorships. Also, Mike often urged the PGA to require teaching pros to take lessons in anatomy and kinesiology, since he thought this was intrinsic to knowing the golf swing.

While Mike despised the PGA as an organization, his emotion toward the PGA swing was even stronger. Several times I asked Mike to describe the difference between his swing and the PGA's. He began his answer with such a tirade of insults against the PGA that it was difficult to extract a straight answer. He would say that the turning of the hips, taught by the PGA, "looks like you're trying to show your asshole to someone on the green." Another time he raged that the pros all had their wrists uncocked at the top of their backswings. Since his answers were so brief and the differences so significant, I've made my own comparison of the two swings based on years of studying both methods.

I have consulted *Swing Like a Pro: The Breakthrough Method of Perfecting Your Golf Swing* by Dr. Ralph Mann and Fred Griffin with Guy Yocom, published in 1998. The book is based on a computer analysis of the swings of pro golfers. The reasoning is that the pro swing is the best swing out there, so of course the reader will want to pattern his or her swing after the pros. On the other hand, I was excited to be patterning my swing after Mike Austin's method, which I felt was superior to the best swing on the professional golf tour.

I picked up *Swing Like a Pro* with some trepidation, fearful that the book would describe what Austin taught as deeply flawed and give valid reasons to support that argument. However, it seemed that the teachings of the book supported many of Austin's principles but didn't go as far as he did. For example, the authors recommend a lateral movement of the hips, but not to the extent that Austin uses this power-generating move. Some of the elements described as essential in *Swing Like a Pro* were completely missing in the Austin swing, leading me to believe that Mike's technique was simpler and, maybe, easier to learn. Perhaps he did a better job of isolating and identifying the necessary actions and eliminating the motions that were superfluous.

Here, then, is the PGA swing in a nutshell.

Golf pros teach their students to turn their hips and shoulders as the club is taken up and back. During the backswing the club is also raised in such a way that the angle between the arms and the club is greatly altered. Consequently, on the downswing this angle must be reestablished at impact to hit the ball accurately.

The downswing begins with a weight shift as the golfer's right elbow returns to the hip. Pros call this motion "dropping the club into the slot." The slot refers to the way that, to maximize power, the club needs to swing back to the ball from a different direction than it was taken away on the backswing. This move of dropping the club into the slot is very difficult for recreational golfers to learn, since in the beginning it feels unnatural. Most amateur golfers never learn to drop the club into the slot—never even attempt it—and play countless rounds of golf during which they hit weak slices.

Another important element of the PGA swing is the rolling of the wrists, first one way on the backswing, and then the other way on the downswing. As the club is taken back, the left wrist rolls over the right wrist. A baseball bat is swung in a very similar way. However, a baseball bat is round and is swung on a different plane than a golf club. The rolling of the wrists causes the blade of the club to fan open on the backswing and roll closed on the downswing.

I spoke with Shauger many times about the Austin swing, and he explained it in such a way that augmented the cryptic nuggets I got from Mike. He said that in the swing that is commonly taught the blade of the club revolves around the shaft. Perfect timing is required to roll the wrists back into the correct position at the moment of impact so that the ball is driven straight toward the target. He said the PGA swing was reliable only for "ball beaters"–golfers who continually tune up their swing at the driving range. This is why Mike says that pros are "playing Russian roulette" when they swing–they never know when the swing will misfire, sending the ball off in the wrong direction.

In the Austin swing the wrists are used in a way that is opposite to what the PGA teaches. The swing begins with the right wrist crossing the left. Done properly, the club goes back on line and turns under and up, remaining square to the ball's line of flight. The hips tilt and then turn, and the left heel is raised to allow weight shift to the point where, at the top of the back-swing, most of the body is behind the ball. The downswing begins with a toss of the club, to start it swinging, and a massive weight shift back to the left.

Let's stop the downswing for a minute to let you fully appreciate the effects of this weight shift. One of Mike's principles, which I haven't heard anywhere else, is that his arms *do not* swing. "It looks like my arms are swinging, but they aren't," he once told me. "My shoulders are turning around my neck, but my arms are not changing in relation to my shoulders." The arms don't swing away from the body until well after the ball is struck.

Shauger used an analogy that really helped me understand the important concept of the non-swinging arms. He said that if a car was towing another car with a rope, the rope had to remain taut to provide pulling power. When the rope was slack, no power was transmitted to the second car. Similarly, if a golfer's arms begin to swing away from his chest, the power of the legs is lost. "You can feel like you have a more powerful swing, because you're working harder," Shauger said. "But actually, power is being siphoned off. You have to redirect your sensitivity away from your arms and feel the power coming from your lower body."

Back to the downswing—if a golfer uses the Austin shift, and has supple wrists, the club is slung into the hitting area at a high speed. As Mike told me, you don't feel you are hitting the ball hard, "but the result is fast hands." As the plaque on Mike's wall said, the power comes from the tilting spine, while the shoulders and wrists are "accelerators." Mike once explained this concept to me by impatiently demanding, "Haven't you ever seen a rocket on the end of a rocket?" The legs are the first stage and the shoulder and hands are the second stage of the rocket, accelerating the clubhead even faster.

So, where does the power come from in the Austin swing? It took me a long time to understand the answer to this question. For years I listened to Mike say how he used the levers of the body to produce maximum power. It always made me think, "That's cool. But exactly how does leverage fit into the golf swing?"

The best way to visualize the leverage in Austin's swing is to

The Spine

The Spine is responsible for more motion of the sketal frame, than it has been credited for. Freedom of 29 kinetic vertebrae allow the spine to rotate 70° laterally, and if desired to bend forward to touch ones toes, without bending the knees.

The Spine accounts for a major force generated in the Golf Swing. The shoulder blades, elbows, and wrists being the accelerators of the golf club.

Mike Austin

The use of the spine is misunderstood by most golfers, according to Mike.

picture the shoulders and spine as looking like a "T"—the shoulders are the top of the T, while the spine is the lower part of the T. If this T was thumb-tacked to the wall at the intersection of the shoulders and the spine, the base of the spine could freely swing back and forth. When the bottom of the spine swings, the shoulders rock. Visualize the left branch of the T (the left shoulder) being connected to your arm, which is, in turn, holding a long golf club. As the downswing begins, the left shoulder is raised. Since it is connected to a long lever, a small motion of the left shoulder moves the clubhead a long way at a high rate of speed. Add to this the acceleration of the relaxed wrists, and you can produce very fast clubhead speed without feeling that you are hitting at the ball with your arms and hands.

One of the teaching points in *Swing Like a Pro* is that the plane of the swing flattens at the top of the backswing. In other words, the club shaft drops as you begin the downswing. This is accomplished by starting the downswing with the lower body while the upper body is still moving backward. I've heard this mentioned in other books, and you can actually see this in many of the pros' swings. After reading about this technique, I used it myself with some success, and it seemed to add some distance to my shots. It's a logical way to put acceleration into the golf swing, since it takes the slack out of your body and stretches it tight as it brings the club back into the hitting area.

I couldn't help but wonder where this motion—or something similar—was in the Austin swing. When I asked Mike about it, I remember his response clearly. I described this move where the lower body drives forward while the upper body is still going back. I told him that many pros use it in their golf swing.

"PGA wants you to turn your body into a goddamned rubber band," he growled.

"So you didn't make this move?" I asked.

"Hell, no," he said, his voice growing angry.

"But they said it gives you more distance and—"

"Let me ask you something," he interrupted. "If you were in Los Angeles and you wanted to go to San Francisco, would you go to San Diego first?"

I laughed. "Well, when you put it that way . . ."

"I mean, why the hell would you go all the way around the world just to go to the shithouse?"

"So you didn't make this move at all? Or anything like it?"

"Why in hell would I do that?" he shouted. "I took the club back. I stopped. I swung it down to the ball."

End of story.

Later, I looked at videos of Mike's swing. Nowhere did I see this recommended move of flattening the club. There was nothing in his swing that was anything like it. As usual, Mike was right. I discarded this move and eliminated it from my practice routine.

To summarize, there are three main differences between the Austin swing and the PGA swing:

1. In the Austin swing the club is taken away so that the face is, as Mike says, "square to the points of the compass throughout the entire swing." If this is done properly, a thin shot or a fat shot could be hit, but the ball will always go straight at where the golfer is aimed.

2. The hips tilt rather than turning. (Some pros, including Ben

Hogan, described a lateral "slide" of the hips.) The tilting of the hips generates more power through leverage, and it prevents the twisting that can injure the spine.

3. The club is thrown from the top of the backswing while the golfer makes a powerful weight shift. This is radically different from the PGA, which tells golfers to drop the club into the slot and delay the release until late in the swing.

If you've been paying attention to all this, a question might have formed in your mind: If the Austin swing is so superior, why wasn't it discovered before? Shauger gave me the answer: "You couldn't discover the Austin swing by accident, because it is counterintuitive. It had to be designed by someone who knew how the joints of the body could be used to produce leverage and maximize clubhead speed. When you fully understand it, you see it's a thing of beauty. Mike Austin is the Leonardo da Vinci of the golf swing."

CHAPTER 10

A CHANGE OF DIRECTION

After the enthusiastic reception of my *Times* article, I felt sure that a book about Mike Austin would be welcomed by golfers everywhere. The most obvious approach was to write an instructional guide explaining how to learn the Austin swing. I asked for Mike's cooperation with such a book and he agreed. We met several times to talk about the swing, and I continued to learn a great deal about his method. However, our conversations kept straying to other subjects. It was hard to avoid delving deeper into his colorful past. While the golfing instruction was essential, the drama of his life held just as much interest for me. Given my dual role as journalist and fiction writer (I had written plays, TV scripts, and novels), I kept picturing his larger-than-life exploits as scenes in a movie or a book. In my mind, Mike Austin was to golf what John Wayne was to Westerns.

Unfortunately, there were other problems with writing an instructional book. For one thing, Mike said he had already written his own book.

"Can I read it?" I asked during one of my visits.

"It's right over there," he said, indicating a stack of papers next to his Barcalounger. I sorted through the various faxes and letters he had received and found a slim manuscript, about seventy pages long and triple-spaced.

"I'd like to take this with me and read it," I said.

"Read it now."

"Here?"

"Yes."

I knew Mike was very protective of anything he had created. That was one of the reasons why he wasn't a household name—he had jealously guarded all of his ideas. If he had taken more risks, and shared his information more freely, I think the word of his accomplishments would have spread widely.

I picked up Mike's manuscript and, with him watching me, began reading. It was precise and clearly worded. Actually it was too precise. It was a series of sentences along the lines of "Put the right knee exactly here" and "Supinate the left wrist as it passes the right thigh" or "Turn the ulna bone in such-and-such direction." This would have been fine if he were teaching golf to a group of doctors who could recognize all the anatomical references. But when I cowrote Dr. Tom Amberry's book on free throw shooting, I broke it into pieces and interspersed the specific mechanics with motivational concepts and anecdotes. Readers told me the book not only showed them how to shoot free throws, but it also made them believe they could do it. A good instructional book should simplify the process and be a joy to read. Mike's book was a bit like a shop manual about rebuilding an automatic transmission.

"I'd really like to take this book to work from," I said. "I can copy it and bring it back."

"That book isn't leaving this house," Mike said firmly. "That's the key, right there. Understand? That's the formula. It's gold."

"Right. But it needs to be presented in a way that people can absorb. After all, we're asking them to make a big change to their game."

"They'll have to change everything," Mike growled.

"And most people want instant results. So they have to be convinced that this is a better way and that they are capable of doing it."

"Let me ask you one thing," Mike said, pointing his finger at me. "If you have cancer, what do you do?"

"Well, it kind of depends, really."

"You cut it out! Cut out the cancer. Ninety-nine percent of the golfers out there have cancer. They have to cut it out to learn my swing."

This was typical of my exchanges with Mike on the subject of golf teaching. But there was another problem I faced in doing an instructional book. I hadn't yet fully grasped and demonstrated the benefits of the Austin swing. While I didn't expect to blast the ball the way Mike had, I wanted to hit the ball with more power and accuracy. In these departments I had experienced great improvement, but I knew that I still had a long way to go. For me to write the book at this point made me feel a little like a fraud. I would be putting things into words that I hadn't personally experienced.

In writing the free throw shooting book I had learned Dr. Tom's method well enough to make 48 free throws in a row—a drop in the bucket compared to Dr. Tom's 2,750 consecutive free throws in twelve hours. Still, I had learned the method well enough to write about it. I still hoped to someday make 100 consecutive free throws, but I had to file that impulse away under "future accomplishments." I idly speculated that I would someday like to accomplish a "100/300 goal"—100 free throws in a row and a drive of 300 yards.

Despite these doubts, I wrote several chapters of an instructional book with Mike. He read and approved the chapters but seemed somewhat unenthusiastic about the project. The response from publishers was also lukewarm. My agent, Robert Wilson, told me that publishers kept telling him that the market was saturated with golf instructional books.

"Even from the world's longest hitter?" I asked him.

"They only want books by Tiger Woods," Rob said.

"But Mike outdrove Tiger by a hundred yards!" I wailed.

"I'm as puzzled as you are," he said. "But this is the market we're dealing with."

That just didn't seem right to me, since I knew there were hundreds of thousands of frustrated golfers out there looking for a better swing, hoping to someday play golf the way the sport was meant to be played.

The book project stalled even though I still felt strongly that golfers needed to know about Mike and his exploits. One day I got a call from my friend Jim Ullrich, who had been with me the first time I met Mike.

"*Pheel?*" he said in his East Texas accent. "How's that Mike Austin book comin' along?"

"I'm stuck," I said and glumly told him how the instructional book had been rejected by a number of publishers.

"Well, shoot, I called just in time," he said, chuckling as if he had a secret he was about to tell me. "I met a fella down here you have to get with. His name is J. B. Hutchens and he played with Mike back in his heyday. He's got stories about Mike you won't hardly believe."

I wanted to ask what difference these stories would make to an instructional book. I had met some of Jim's friends, and they were all colorful old boys with nicknames like "Red Dog." But to humor him, I called "J. B." to see what he knew about Mike.

The first thing I learned was that the man's name was actually Jay B. Hutchens. He had been a pro at the Memorial Park Golf Course for many years, starting in 1947. He remembered playing in several tournaments with Mike and got to know him somewhat over the years. But the first thing that really caught my attention was the way that Hutchens had first met Mike.

"I was playing a tournament in Houston one year," Hutchens

recalled, "and I had just hit my best drive of the day. I boomed it way out there. I walked to my ball, hit my second shot, and walked *at least* a hundred yards when here came this ball from behind me. I turned around and saw that it was Mike Austin's tee shot. I had no idea anyone could hit the ball to that spot on the golf course. It seemed impossible."

As Hutchens watched Mike play, he said that his swing always looked like he was laying up. "But when you saw where the ball went, you knew he wasn't laying up. He was going for it." Hutchens said that he had also seen renowned long-hitter George Bayer play in local tournaments but thought that Mike could hit it much farther. Bayer's *New York Times* obituary said, "At 6 feet 5 inches and 230 pounds, Bayer hit drives exceeding 300 yards at a time of wooden clubs and low-technology golf balls. He once set a record, later surpassed, with a tournament drive of 436 yards." Later, when I asked Mike about Bayer he said he had given Bayer golf lessons. "He could hit it a long way." Mike recalled. "But you never knew where the damn ball was going to go. He was all over the golf course."

The other thing I remember Hutchens telling me was that Mike enjoyed going to the driving range at a tournament and attracting a crowd that would *oooo* and *ahhh* while he hit drives. He joked with the spectators and was very friendly. Everyone seemed to like him.

Strange, I thought. This isn't the picture of Mike I had in my mind from hearing his stories of fistfights and other confrontations. Maybe, as Dr. Tom had once observed, his personality was greatly changed by the stroke, altering his behavior by 180 degrees.

"But if Mike could hit the ball so well, why didn't he win more tournaments?" I asked Hutchens.

"This is just the impression I got, okay? But I'd have to say it just wasn't his thing. To win a tournament you had to really buckle down and score. Of course, he couldn't putt, but he didn't seem really interested in that part of the game. He played tournaments to meet people and show off his great swing. He was a big handsome guy, and he was a real hit with the women, believe me. No, I think Mike was just out there to have fun."

After I hung up, I felt my mind repainting my mental portrait of Mike Austin. And I began to wonder how many other people out there had memories about Mike whom I hadn't heard from yet.

And then it hit me. I could write a book that analyzed Mike's character *and* his golf swing. The swing description could be interspersed with stories from Mike's life, a life of contrast and contradiction, starting with this one—the game's longest hitter never learned to putt. It wouldn't be a straight-ahead how-to book, but it would increase golfers' understanding of the swing. And I would verify the method by reaching my goal of hitting a 300-yard drive. In the book I would present Mike the way I came to know him, crusty, generous, difficult, funny, and always surprising.

I began writing.

Almost immediately I knew I was on the right track. This was the book I wanted to write all along. One thing made me a little nervous, though. I had decided it was important to present Mike exactly as I had known him, complete with all the rough edges. How would he react to this? I couldn't help but remember his stories of the fights he had won. Would he lure me close to his chair and then deck me with a single punch? I remembered how he had been demonstrating the correct hand action as I leaned over his chair. I looked into his pale eyes as he said, "Hell, I could break your goddamned scapula with this action. Just like this, *BAM!*"

It was stories like this that gave me a great deal of respect for Mike's opinions. Ultimately, though, I decided that I would be guided by one thought: If it were true, I would write it. If Mike protested, my defense would be to ask him if it really happened. I was banking on the hope that Mike's honest streak would save my neck.

Now that the course of the book had changed direction, I needed to gather more material from him. Once again I dialed his number. The phone rang. Once, twice, three times. In the past he had always picked up the phone immediately, answering in his firm voice with the slight Scottish accent. A frightening thought flickered through my mind: What if he had died? He was, after all, ninety-two years old by now. Even Mike Austin couldn't live forever. Finally, his answering machine

Mike's penetrating gaze made his critics squirm.

picked up and I left a message. He called me back a few minutes later, explaining that he had been in the bathroom. I was relieved to hear from him. But my fear of his death lingered with me for days, and I knew that when he did pass away I would miss him. It was then that I realized he was no longer just source material for stories. He was a friend.

CHAPTER 11

DIGGING DEEPER INTO THE PAST

The next week, on my way to visit Mike and begin the new version of my book, I called him on my cell phone to tell him I was going to be a little late. He asked me if I wouldn't mind stopping at the store for him, because he had a clogged sink and needed some drain cleaner. I agreed, and while I was in the grocery store I also bought some cinnamon rolls, since it was late in the afternoon and my stomach was rumbling.

When I walked in the door, I found Mike fiddling with the remote for his VCR. He finished setting the recorder, put the remote aside, and the light fell on his face for the first time. His skin looked waxy and drawn, his eyes were hooded and pulled down at the corners. But his posture in the chair, as always, was ramrod straight.

"I got your drain cleaner," I said. "Want me to pour some in the sink?"

"Would you do that, please?" he said. "I'd do it myself, but I don't want to get up. And here, pay yourself back." He handed me a money clip holding together a large wad of bills, some of them hundreds. For some reason, I got the feeling he wanted to show he trusted me to take what I needed to pay myself back and leave his money untouched.

"Thanks, Mike." I pulled off a few singles and handed the wad back to him. "Hey, I brought us some cinnamon rolls. Want one now?"

"Hell, yes," he said, brightening up. "Let's have some coffee to go with it. I know you like coffee. Can you work the coffee maker in there yourself?"

"I'll figure it out."

I poured the chemical drain cleaner into the bathroom sink. Then I began making coffee. From the other room I heard him say, "I've been having a little trouble getting out of my chair. Then, the other day I had a fall. They took me into the hospital and checked me out."

I paused with the coffee pot under the sink, my hand on the faucet. "Did they find anything?"

"They said there's a valve in my abdominal artery that isn't working, so not enough blood is flowing to my legs. They want to put a shunt into the artery to keep the blood flowing."

"Is that a serious operation?" I asked, coming back into the living room.

"They'll slice me right down the center and pull the damn thing right out, snip it, and put that shunt in," Mike said, illustrating with his hands where the cut would be made and how the operation would be performed. "I've got a surgeon who is highly recommended. Then maybe my legs will start working again, but it must be circulating okay, because I'm not addle-brained."

I laughed. "No, I'd never describe you as addle-brained. You can remember your score on every round of golf you've ever played. And you remember what everyone else shot too."

Mike chuckled in a sort of a low, machine-gun rattle. When something really tickled him, particularly something mischievous, like a dirty joke, he had this way of chuckling—almost cackling—that was oddly infectious.

I brought him a mug of coffee and a cinnamon roll and turned on my tape recorder. "I wanted to ask you a few more questions about your family," I said. I had decided to treat the material Mike gave me for the *Times* article as the first layer of information. These were the stock answers he gave to questions people often asked him. I wondered what lay under the surface—and more importantly, what Mike's feelings were about the remarkable life he had led. This was the perfect day for these questions; for once the phone wasn't ringing off the hook, and Tanya was out playing golf. The house was quiet and, for the first time, it was just Mike and me.

"I get the impression that your father was a very impressive person," I said. "Did you have a close relationship with him?"

"No," Mike admitted. "I always had the feeling that he didn't have time for me. I was the youngest—I had two older sisters, who were very musical, and two older brothers. My oldest brother,

Needham, was eight years older than me. He was incredibly handsome with chiseled features. He was my father's pride and joy and he took him everywhere. He never did take me anywhere with him."

"Was your brother a golfer?"

"Both of my brothers could have been pros," he said. "But my oldest brother was only interested in women."

"Really?"

"When he was only fifteen, fancy cars used to pull up in front of our house and he would get out. If you looked inside you'd see a rich woman, maybe twenty-seven or twenty-eight years old. See, my brother could make any woman, just by looking at her. Women couldn't resist him. Finally my father said, 'I won't have you setting a bad example for my daughters. If you do that again, you're out.'"

"So he stopped?"

"No. About a week later a woman brought him home in a Stutz. My father ran him off at only fifteen years old. And he didn't want to let him back into the family."

"What happened to him?"

"He lived with this woman who was very wealthy, and she put him through college. She died and left him all her money. So he started a charter boat business, bringing people from Miami to Tampa and back. When he was about twenty-seven years old, he was coming back for a family reunion—it was the first time he would have been back—he hit a pole going about eighty miles per hour. The pole broke off and went right through the center of his chest and killed him instantly."

It was very quiet in the room for a moment. It was that intense kind of quiet where two people are sharing a moment, each interpreting it their own way. For my part I was picturing Mike's brother looking like F. Scott Fitzgerald, painfully handsome, with slicked-back hair and a high collar. Mike was probably recalling a thousand memories of his older brother, a brother he surely idolized. I won't say that Mike sounded choked up about his brother's death—the events he described were so far in the past he had come to terms with them. But it was his father's neglect that seemed to have opened a wound. I couldn't help wondering whether these early feelings of inadequacy, of needing to impress his father, had stayed with him. Maybe he had spent his life desperately trying to achieve something that would earn his father's admiration—even after the man died. It reminded me of something that Mike Dunaway once said: "I can describe Mike Austin in three words—*in the world*. In everything he does he wants to be the best *in the world*."

Much later, I learned something about Mike, and his relationship with his brother, that surprised me. Mike, his wife, and I were talking about a boat Mike owned, that he used to pilot to Catalina Island, off the coast of Southern California. Almost casually, Tanya said, "You know, Mike never learned to swim."

I was completely shocked. Mike, the ultimate athlete, not being able to swim! It seemed impossible.

"Why didn't you learn?" I asked.

"I never overcame my fear of water."

"Where did your fear come from?"

"My oldest brother used to hold me out over the water," Mike said. "He told me he was going to drop me in. I was terrified. And I never got over it."

I drank my coffee in silence for a few moments, thinking about how cruel older brothers can be. I was the second oldest in my family of four. I had an older sister and two younger brothers. I wondered what scars I might have left on my younger brothers.

"What about your other brother?" I asked. "What was he like?"

"His name was Joseph Lafayette Austin, Jr. He never opened a schoolbook, never studied—and he still got straight A's," Mike said. "At the age of twenty-one he was the head of the Atlanta Stock Exchange. But when he was still very young he said he wanted to die."

"What? Why?"

"He said, 'Hell, I feel like I've been here before. I can go into any city in America, and even though I've never been there I can tell you what it looks like.' He proved it to me too. I guess he was psychic. He told me that life on this earth was boring. Nothing was new to him. I never figured out what gave him that insight, but you know what? I have it too."

"You're psychic," I said.

"Yes," he nodded. "I know things before they happen."

I had seen this bizarre side to Mike before. He occasionally went off on tangents about his theories on the origin of the universe, about interplanetary travel, and about how he wanted to create a separate nation under the sea called "Aqualandia." But as I said, I had never known Mike to lie, so I never completely discounted what he said. Besides, I actually believe the mind is so mysterious that some people might possess psychic abilities. If anyone were psychic, it struck me that it would be someone as brilliant as Mike.

"Give me an example of your psychic ability," I said.

"I worked intelligence for the U.S military during World War Two and I had to interrogate spies. I could always tell what they were thinking. People can't lie to me."

"Can I try lying to you and see if you can catch me?" I asked.

He let out that chuckle again. It was his only answer. He never seemed surprised by my suspicion—I guess he was used to people's skepticism, since he had done so many incredible things to be skeptical about.

"Can you give me another example?" I asked Mike.

"Golfers would come out to California on the tour. They'd run out of money or gamble their money away. Then they'd come to me for a loan. I was known as the person who helped out the struggling golfers."

"You loaned them the money they asked for?"

"Gave them the money. I had to. I could look into the future and see what would happen if I didn't. I didn't want to let them ruin their lives. I put old women in homes, I put young people through college. Then, when they paid me back I didn't cash the checks. I have a drawer full of checks over there I never cashed."

I wanted to get up and check the drawer he indicated. But I just accepted his story and kept my seat.

"You said you did intelligence work for the U.S. in the war," I said, "but you told me once you were in the British Air Force." It was this kind of inconsistency that always made me wonder if Mike made things up. As usual, he had an answer.

"When my family came to this country from England, we didn't take out citizenship. No one cared until the War came, and then the State Department sent us to Canada. They were advertising for flyers, so I enlisted. I wanted to go to France, but they sent me to Africa." There, Mike was made a wing commander in the British Air Force and conducted intelligence operations for the Americans. He flew a DC-3 cargo plane, ostensibly filled with supplies though the boxes were actually empty—if he went down in enemy territory it was hoped the enemy wouldn't realize he was on a covert mission.

Mike then launched into a long, complicated story about a German submarine anchored off the coast of Africa that was intercepting information about Allied troop movements. Unfortunately, the story was hard to follow, but I remember it involved General Bernard Montgomery, a beautiful woman, a knockout drug, and the eventual capture of the submarine crew. Sometime later, flying his DC-3 over Nigeria, the engines failed and he prepared to make a crash landing. As he lost altitude he saw what he thought was an open field in the distance. He had no choice but to put it down there. Unfortunately, it turned out to be a swamp. He wound up in the water, his legs broken and crocodiles swimming all around him. One crocodile swam right up between his legs and, he said, "My blood went cold—it absolutely congealed."

Because of the wounds Mike suffered in the plane crash, and his intelligence work for the American forces, he was awarded U.S. citizenship. He was given leave and returned to Los Angeles, his legs still in braces.

At this point we were interrupted by the sound of the front door opening. Tanya came in. She came in wearing her golfing clothes, and the smell of the outdoors seemed to cling to her as she walked into the room. She greeted us cheerfully.

"I recorded that program you wanted," Mike told her.

"Oh, thank you for remembering," she said, putting her things away.

"I had a hell of a time working the recorder, but I think I got it," he said, picking up the remote. "Do you want to watch it now?"

"After dinner."

"Anytime you want to watch it just let me know," Mike said. "I'll set it up for you."

I was a little surprised to see Mike treating Tanya so delicately. Usually, he was pretty demanding and brusque. I couldn't help but wonder what had changed. Tanya sat down with us and began chatting about the early days in Hollywood when she and Mike would go to what later became known as "Muscle Beach" in Venice, California, on the west side of Los Angeles. Tanya pulled out a picture of Mike and his two deeply tanned friends. Because of Mike's near-albino skin color he looked incredibly pale. "He was as white as a milk bottle," she said.

Seeing Mike and Tanya together I realized there was something I had never asked them before. "How did you two meet?"

Their answer came in little bits of dialogue, one supplying a detail from their point of view, the other echoing with their own memory. It was touching, a little like two musicians playing a duet.

While he was overseas, Mike had made money on the side by buying and selling liquor and cigarettes. He sent the money home from Africa to a friend who put it in a safe-deposit box. After he returned to Los Angeles in 1945, just before the end of the War, Mike went to visit the friend, who lived in Venice. He went to the friend's house and was told that his friend was down at the beach. He walked down there, still wearing his uniform and the leg braces from the plane crash. He met his friend but also spotted a woman sitting on a beach blanket nearby.

"Who's that girl?" Mike asked his friend.

"That's my sister," his friend said rather protectively.

"Well, tell your sister to come over here. I want to meet her," Mike said.

Tanya took over the story at this point. "I saw Mike come down to the beach in his uniform, and I thought, 'He's the one for me.' But I was shy, so I jumped into the water and went swimming."

Tanya, whose maiden name was Somova, was the daughter of Russian immigrants who had originally landed in New York City before journeying west. She was an aspiring actress and stunt woman who lived in a boardinghouse in Hollywood where many other movie hopefuls—one of them Marilyn Monroe—lived. When Mike went to call on Tanya, all the other girls in the boardinghouse told their troubles to Mike. According to Tanya, he sat patiently and listened to their problems for hours.

"That was the happiest time," Tanya said. She looked questioningly at Mike as if looking for agreement. He was silent, so she added, "For me, anyway."

When they were first married, Tanya had no interest in learning golf. But several years later she agreed to take lessons from Mike so they could play together. When he became impatient and yelled at her, she said, she would cry. But eventually she became an excellent golfer and they won many pro-lady-am (professional and lady amateur) tournaments together. "He drove for show and I putted for the dough," she said, laughing.

Rather than return to active duty overseas, Mike was sent to work on a special government research project in Gardena, south of Los Angeles. Their work centered on the development of liquid and solid fuels used in rocket propulsion. There, he became acquainted with the properties of different metals, which eventually helped him develop and design his golf clubs.

As I listened to Mike and Tanya talking, I once again felt there was something different in the air, a tone I'd never heard in Mike's voice before. I couldn't figure out what it was.

During one of the pauses Mike suddenly said, "Tanya, I talked to the surgeon again."

"Who?"

"The surgeon who's going to perform my operation tomorrow."

"Oh, yes."

"He's a brilliant man. Everyone I talk to says he's the best."

"I'm sure he is," Tanya said, patting Mike's leg. "You'll be fine."

Suddenly, it hit me, and I knew what was different—it seemed like Mike was afraid of tomorrow's operation. Despite the way he had described the procedure, bravely showing me how he would be sliced open, and which organs would be removed and which artery would be snipped, he was afraid of what might happen. He was afraid he might die or become completely incapacitated.

At that moment, I was like a kid who realizes that his father is not really a superman—that he is mortal and someday he will die. Here was my hero looking at the great beyond, hesitating and saying, "I'm not ready to go."

For some reason, I recalled a story a friend had told me once while we were sharing a bottle of wine. One day my friend's heart suddenly began hammering wildly and he couldn't slow it down. In the emergency room the nurse said they would have to give him an injection that would stop his heart briefly and then the doctors would restart his heart so it would beat regularly again. My friend said he had grabbed the nurse's arm and pleaded with her, saying, "Don't make me go into the dark! I'm not ready for the dark!"

Now, here was Mike, pondering tomorrow's operation and sounding nervous. Was it possible that my hero, Mike Austin, was human after all? But if he was, I really didn't want to know it. I'd rather keep him as a superhero, someone who would spit in death's eye and live forever.

We had been talking for several hours and it was time for me to leave. I stood up and bent over Mike's chair, taking his left hand in both of mine.

"I have to go now, Mike," I said. "But I'll give you a call and see how the operation went. I'm sure you'll be fine."

"Yes, well, the surgeon's a great man," Mike said. "Everyone says he's the best in the field."

"I'm sure he is. I'll come again soon."

I began to walk out the door. But then I paused. Now, I was the one feeling nervous about his operation. It was dawning on me that the day would come when I would walk out this door for the last time. And I wasn't ready for that to happen. I was tempted to try to say something to Mike, but I didn't know how to put my feelings into words. I turned and found Mike sitting in his chair watching me. He seemed to sense what I was thinking, and he held my eyes as if to say he understood. I waved to him. He raised his hand in a half-salute.

Chapter 12

The Happiest Time

Two days later I took my cellular phone and ducked out of my office at Edmunds.com in Santa Monica. I shared an office with another writer, and I didn't want to disturb him with my phone conversation. I stepped onto a patio outside the company's lunchroom. It had rained the night before and all the chairs were still wet, so I had to stand as I dialed, leaning on a railing that looked over a courtyard. The sun was coming out, warming the air, and everything around me looked clean and beautiful. Moments like this made me glad I lived in California.

I punched in Mike's number and expected that his answering machine would pick up. I assumed he was still in the hospital recuperating from the operation. However, the phone was answered after the first ring.

"Mike Austin," came the clear, firm voice, although it sounded a little subdued.

"Hey, Mike, it's Phil."

"Hello, buddy," he said. His enthusiasm seemed a bit muted.

"I called to see how the operation went."

"I didn't have it," he said, and added nothing more.

Finally, I asked, "Why? What happened?"

"They examined me again, and the doctor decided that if they operated on me it would kill me. So they sent me home." He sounded tired and disappointed.

"So, what's going to happen?" I asked.

"The doctor said I could live another month, I could live a year—there's no way of telling." He paused, and then added, "So I'll just live until I die."

It was a strange way to put it—*I'll just live until I die.* I knew what he meant. And yet it also seemed paradoxical.

"That's what we're all doing," I said, hoping to cheer him up. And then I said what I always did, "You know, you're sounding great."

"Thanks, buddy. I'll just have to see what happens."

We chatted for a few minutes, talking about my recent rounds of golf. I asked him a few questions about my swing, which he answered in the concise, passionate way he had answered similar questions many times before. The subject of golf always restored his spirits, and after a few minutes his voice was strong again.

"Mike, I'm at work now so I have to go," I said. "I'll stop by again soon."

"Any time," he said. "Come by any time. And I want you to know something."

"Yes."

"I've enjoyed our association," he said.

I was about to reply in a similar way, that I had enjoyed knowing him too. But I didn't want to put our relationship in the past tense. I didn't want to give him the feeling that I thought our "association," as he put it so formally, would soon be ending. Instead, I said, "I'm glad I've gotten to know you. We'll get together again soon and do more work on the book."

"I'd like that," he said, brightening up a little. "Come any time. Good-bye—and God bless you."

That phrase, "I've enjoyed our association," was a sobering reminder that our time together was limited. I've noticed that people sometimes have a sixth sense, almost an animal instinct, of their impending death. Mike seemed to be concluding his life, tying up loose ends before he left, paying his last respects. Every time I talked to him, I had begun feeling it might be the last time, so I called him twice a week.

Once, I called him while I was driving home. My commute lasts an hour in the afternoon, and when I'm stuck in traffic it's a nice private time for me to talk to my family and friends. And so I called Mike from my car on my cell phone. He was almost always in his chair, watching the Golf Channel, and it was reassuring to hear his voice answer in his characteristic way.

These calls to Mike weren't easy. He had never been, and never would be, a comfortable guy to be around. But if I have a gift, it is the ability to talk to a wide range of people, to make people feel relaxed and get them to open up. Some years previously, while ghostwriting Allen Funt's autobiography, I had listened to him describe how he had created the legendary TV show *Candid Camera*. He told me, "Everyone has a story to tell. If you can't get them to tell it, it's because you haven't asked the right question."

With these thoughts in mind, I decided I would call Mike and just relax as much as possible while we talked. I would let him initiate, bring up topics for discussion if he wanted to, or just let a moment or two pass in silence if that's how things went. I wouldn't compulsively fire questions at him just to avoid uncomfortable lapses in conversation.

"Well, buddy," Mike said when he heard it was me calling. "It's good to hear your voice. Are you in Santa Monica now?"

"No, actually, I'm on my way home. I just thought I'd see how you are doing."

"I feel fine," he said. "I've even figured out a way to walk again. See, what I do is—" And in great detail he told me how he locked this knee and moved this joint and swung this leg forward (even though it was paralyzed) and was able to walk. I was amazed at both his spirit and his sheer engineering ability to trick his worn-out old body into answering his commands. It also reminded me of how he once told me he had escaped from the hospital after an operation, driving his Cadillac with a bed sheet twisted around his foot so that he could bend his leg into position to reach the gas pedal.

"You know, Mike," I said, "You're really sounding full of energy."

"You always sound full of energy," Mike answered. It was one of the few times he had said anything about me. I was a little startled. "How're you hitting 'em?"

"I've been swinging the Flammer every day," I said. "It straightens me right out."

"That Flammer is the best damn practice device on the market," Mike said, getting that competitive edge in his voice. "Hell, I just had a dentist call me. He bought a Flammer last week, went out today and hit the ball two hundred and eighty-seven yards. He called me, told me he'd never hit the ball that far in his entire life."

"Is he a big guy?" I asked.

"Hell, no. He's short, bald, and left-handed."

I couldn't help laughing at that. And Mike laughed too, cackling wickedly as he realized what he had said.

We talked about this and that, and suddenly he asked, "Do you have a large family?" His voice sounded almost wistful. I was a little startled since, in our years of knowing each other, he had never asked me about my family and I had never brought it up.

"I'm married, and I have two boys. I have a sixteen-year-old and a twelve-year-old. They really keep me busy."

"I'd like to meet them. Would you bring them over sometime?"

"Sure."

I was anticipating that Mike would ask me if either of my sons played golf. I was ready to brag about how my older son, Andrew, got a hole-in-one when he was only nine years old playing at Hartwell Golf Course in Long Beach. But for some reason, I heard myself saying, "My older son's passion is music."

"That's wonderful," Mike sighed. "I know that for me, the happiest moments of my life have been while I've been singing. My music has taken me all over the world. I loved opera, but I used to love singing Irish folk ballads the best." He named an Irish folk tune I'd never heard of and asked me if I knew it.

"I don't think I do," I said.

I heard Mike clear his throat and I realized he was going to sing for me. I felt a wave of embarrassment sweep over me, wondering how I would react to this. But then I remembered that this was a conversation where I would not compulsively try to control things. So I took a deep breath, and as I drove through rush-hour traffic, Mike's rich, deep voice filled my ear. His voice cracked at times and I could feel him groping for long-unused lyrics. But he put all of his heart into the singing; while driving through rush hour traffic, I was touched.

When he finished, I said, "That's so beautiful. The Irish seem to have some of the most haunting songs."

"That's because they've lost their homeland and are in a constant state of sadness," he said. It was an unexpected observation. But then I thought of Mike and the life he had led: born in England, raised in Scotland, then New England, then the Deep South. And finally, moving to Los Angeles. He might certainly understand the heartache that comes from leaving home time after time.

I had always wondered why Mike and Tanya had never had children. And now, with all this talk of families, and children, it seemed like the time to ask. But how could I phrase the question diplomatically?

"Did you ever want children?"

"Yes. But I couldn't have them. You see, when I was in Africa, during World War Two, I contracted a condition called 'Fever X.' They called it Fever X because they never found out what it was. I was one of twenty-eight soldiers who got the disease, and I was the only one who survived. But it prevented me from having children."

Fever X from Africa? The only known survivor? Rendered unable to father children? This was another classic Mike Austin story. At that moment, I felt fortunate to have a family. And I felt sorry for Mike, childless in his final days.

Before we signed off, he said, "I'd like you to bring those boys by here sometime. I want to meet them. Would you do that, please?"

I said I'd bring both my boys up to see him. But I knew even at that time that I probably wouldn't. My sons, Tony and Andrew, wouldn't fit the mold of what Mike was looking for. Besides that, I was afraid one of them would pick up a golf club and Mike would try to teach them how to swing it. I didn't want to put my sons in that awkward position.

"Well, it's been good talking with you," I said, bringing the conversation to a close.

"It's always a pleasure to hear from you, buddy," he said. "And I want you to know something. I love you like a brother."

I was absolutely unprepared for this. And I didn't know how to respond. I think I said something like, "Thank you, Mike. I love you too," but I'm not actually certain. My own feelings of love were clouded by the discomfort of saying that word out loud. For me, *love* is such a big word—the biggest—and I have a lot of trouble saying it. Still, I did love Mike—or at least admired him and respected him. He had helped me grow and eventually, I hoped, reach goals far above what I had thought possible. As he prepared himself to leave this earth, the good he did for others would be carried on through me, and through the other people whose lives he had touched.

After we hung up and I reflected on our conversation about love, I remembered something that happened about ten years ago, just before Christmas. I was rewriting a script with a movie producer and we went out to scout locations. As the producer drove me home, we began talking about our families, since we both had sons the same age. I remember him saying, "What I like about having a son is that it gives me whole new avenue for love." It was awkwardly phrased, but in its awkwardness I felt his sincerity. He dropped me off, and on Christmas Eve I got a phone call—my friend had died of a massive heart attack.

His comment about love, which was virtually the last exchange we had, was frozen in my mind.

Now, at the opposite end of the age spectrum, I found that Mike "loved me like a brother." I was amazed that my feelings—and our relationship—had changed so dramatically since I first met him. My initial reaction to Mike had been skepticism, suspicion, and fear. I never guessed that the day would come when the word *love* would be used between us. Sadly, it made me wonder how many other avenues for love I had missed in my life.

Phil Reed with his hero, Mike Austin.

A week later, just before Christmas, I was hurrying to get ready for a trip to Lake Tahoe with my wife. I had written the required Christmas cards to my family and a few close friends, but I still had a number of cards left unwritten to some business connections. Reviewing the list in my mind, I decided I just didn't have the time to write these cards.

Then, strangely, I felt there was one card that I did need to write—one card that was important enough despite the frantic preparations for our trip and all the other Christmas activities. I chose a cheerful Christmas card and sat with my pen over the paper, composing a message. But I found that a message had already composed itself in my mind. Here is what I wrote:

Dear Mike:

I've enjoyed my visits to see you this year and our many long conversations. I think you are the most remarkable man I've ever met and I consider myself very lucky to know you. Have a wonderful Christmas and I'll look forward to seeing you again in the New Year.

With Best Wishes,

Phil

After I mailed the card, I felt somehow purged. I moved forward with holiday planning and didn't think much about what

I had done. A few days later, presumably when Mike received my card, I got a phone message.

"Hello, buddy. This is old Mike Austin. Merry Christmas, Phil. I wish you a happy new year, a prosperous new year, and a healthy new year. I hope all the things you wish to come true this year will happen for you. Via con Dios, buddy. Go with God."

CHAPTER 13

A DIVINELY ORDAINED SWING

For the next four months my literary agent circulated the first seventy pages of a manuscript I had written about Mike that was then titled "The Greatest Swing." The first few readings of the material brought enthusiastic responses from editors but no firm offers. I kept Mike posted on the manuscript's progress with occasional phone calls, but to tell the truth, I needed to take some time away from the project and gain a better perspective on it. One problem was that I didn't know the ending to my own story. Would I eventually learn the Austin swing and reach my 300-yard goal? My progress toward that benchmark once again seemed stalled. And what about Mike—would his health continue to deteriorate? After the scare about his cancelled operation, he seemed to stabilize and return to his normal state of health. I didn't realize it at the time, but looking back, I see that life was weaving this story's ending on its own, since this was, after all, reality and not one of my fictional stories that I could control.

At some point during this time, I took my sons, Tony and

Andrew, up to Mike's house for a visit. Tony, my younger son, had watched Mike's instructional video and had become fascinated with him, picking up on my frequent assertions that he was a real sports legend. When we went to the driving range, Tony would occasionally belt out Mike Austin phrases he had picked up from the video, astonishing other golfers around him. "It's a circular motion—not a linear motion!" Tony would quote Mike. And other times, after nailing a good drive, Tony would sing out, "Now that's what you call slugging the ball, *mun!*"

When Mike saw my sons walk through his door, his eyes seemed to glow with happiness and excitement. "You're going to be a big *mun!*" he said to Andrew, who had just turned seventeen at the time. I'm happy to say that Andrew, at five feet, ten inches, is taller than his old man, but I don't think he'll get much bigger—no, he won't be big physically. What Mike really meant was that Andrew carried all the hope and promise of youth. Then, looking at Tony, Mike said to me, "You've got two of the handsome-ist boys I've ever seen!"

Mike served the boys soft drinks and sat them on his couch. He then proceeded to tell them all his best stories of the fistfights he had been in and the great golf shots he had hit while playing against the legends of the sport. Andrew didn't know what to make of these stories; Tony listened with wide-eyed enthusiasm. It wasn't exactly the touching encounter I had pictured, but it was all worth it to see the look on Mike's face the first moment he saw my sons. Tony's enthusiasm for Mike remained undaunted—he kept asking me when we could go up and see "Iron Mike" again.

But we didn't go up to see Mike again. And I didn't move forward with the manuscript for many months. During this time I think Mike was a little hurt by my lack of attention.

One Sunday afternoon I was sitting on the couch, watching a golf tournament on TV and, of course, thinking about Mike, when the phone rang. I picked it up and was startled to hear Mike's familiar voice. I remembered our discussion about his psychic powers, and I wondered if he could have telepathically known I was thinking about him.

"How ya doin', buddy?" he said, sounding very chipper. "I sure would like you to stop by the house sometime. I've found a whole bunch of new clippings and photos to show you."

I made the usual excuses—work, family, other time constraints— and promised I would come by soon.

A few days later, Mike called me again at my office and said that Mike Dunaway would be visiting him on Saturday. "You've got to see this invention that he's developed," Mike told me. "It's going to revolutionize golf training. If you have the Flammer and Dunaway's machine, you're going to have all you need to build your swing."

I checked my schedule and agreed to visit him that Saturday. It was a fairly easy drive up to Mike's house that day, particularly since I was behind the wheel of a brand-new BMW 760Li V-12 that I was test-driving for Edmunds.com. I carefully parked the expensive car in front of Mike's house on Irondale and walked up to the front door. It was already in the high nineties, and the heat was still building. In the front yard was Mike's ancient video camera, the teaching mat, and his chair. I assumed that Dunaway would be the student today, although I felt the old tightening of the stomach thinking that he might instead put me in the hot seat.

Inside, I found Mike not with Dunaway but talking with Danny Shauger. Danny had a laptop open and was tapping away while Mike sat in the Barcalounger. Mike looked as alert as always, but his skin was pale and his eyes were hooded. He introduced me to Danny, who stood up and said, "We talked once before on the phone." I remembered the call well. He had told me two things that really stuck with me. He had said that, being a street kid, Mike had been the only real father he had ever known. The other thing I remember him saying was that "Mike Austin is a genius, but you have to be a genius to under-stand what he is saying."

"What happened to Mike Dunaway?" I asked, wondering if I had been teased into coming to visit with the promise of finally meeting the legendary long-ball hitter that Mike had coached.

"He's been delayed down south," Mike said. "He'll be here in a couple of hours. And let me tell you, this swing trainer he's got is going to be worth millions!"

I settled in for the long wait.

"Did Mike tell you about the book we're writing?" Danny asked.

"It's an instruction book?" I asked, remembering my own attempt at writing a golf instructional with Mike.

"Correct," Danny said, removing his reading glasses. "I've been sitting here with Mike the last three weeks trying to get everything down on paper."

"Let me tell you," Mike said, gesturing vigorously. "This book will be better than any book ever written. All the other books have the same old crap. Those people don't know what the hell they're talking about. But this book is the secret, understand?"

Yes, yes, I thought. *I've heard all this before.* Still, I was intrigued with the idea that a golf instructor who had taught Mike Austin's method with such success had now tackled the project.

Danny said he had met Mike, taken lessons, and then become a regular playing partner and occasional caddy. While playing and talking with Mike, he gradually acquired the knowledge to teach the Austin swing at the golf course in Griffith Park. There, he had met Ricky Leech, the singer who had invited Mike to the opera the night he had met Lou Lebherz. He told me he had now cut back to about ten students, one of whom was a young, athletic twenty-six-year-old named Jaacob Bowden. Jaacob was now out on the long-drive tour after being shown the Mike Austin method and increasing his driving distance by over 100 yards. "And he doesn't have the whole method yet!" Danny added excitedly.

Mike and Danny were so enthusiastic that they kept reading me parts of their book from the laptop screen. I was doubtful at first, since I had already read Mike's manuscript and found it to be a dry list of directions. However, the excerpts Danny read sounded solid and well constructed. Danny had a good way of using analogies to convey a series of motions that would have taken much longer to break into pieces. I felt that golf needed to be taught specifically and generally in the same book. An action should be described but then followed up with an image to blend it all together. After all, once the swing is learned, it will have to be so deeply ingrained into muscle memory that when playing, the golfer shouldn't have to think of it at all.

"Do you think you can help us out with our project?" Mike asked. I was surprised by this request, since Mike rarely asked for anything from anyone. But I felt that because of the *Times* article I had written, Mike respected my abilities as a writer.

"Here's what I'd like to do," I said. "I'll edit your book if Danny is willing to spend some time at the driving range with me. I need someone to look at my swing."

I wondered if Mike would resent me working with a different teacher, but he didn't seem concerned. "Danny will get you straightened out," was all he said. "And you can help us with the book."

Danny put the manuscript of his book on a disk, and I put it in my briefcase to read later. A few minutes later the phone rang. Mike snatched it off the hook and spoke to someone.

Apparently, Dunaway was delayed again. When Mike hung up he was chuckling in that mischievous way of his.

"These people talking to Dunaway about his machine are just drooling over it," he said. "He's going to make millions off this thing!"

We decided to go out to lunch while we were waiting for Dunaway to arrive. Danny helped Mike out of his chair and walked him outside to my test car. Mike admired the sleek, gleaming BMW.

"Now this is what I call riding in style," Mike said with a big grin. "What is this?"

"A BMW 760Li with the V-12 engine," I told him.

"What'll it do?" he wanted to know.

"Most of the German cars are electronically governed at a hundred and fifty miles per hour. But without the governor on it, the car could go a lot faster."

He chuckled and shook his head, "One hundred and fifty miles an hour. That was my swing speed back in nineteen thirty-nine."

Mike slowly worked his way into the front seat. Danny had to raise one of Mike's legs up and into the car and then help him swivel around so he could face forward. I fired up the BMW and we headed off for lunch. Something about what Mike had just said didn't ring true.

"How did you know what your swing speed was?" I asked. "They didn't have radar back then."

"I was playing in a tournament in Chicago. They took one hundred golfers over to the University of Illinois to measure their swing speed. They used a board thirty feet wide and forty feet high with lines drawn in six-inch increments and a strobe light. By counting off the different squares my club passed over, in between each flash of the strobe, they could tell how fast I was swinging."

I had never heard of such a thing, but once Mike explained it, it made perfect sense. Once again, any doubts I had about Mike were answered.

"Okay," I said. "So how fast was your clubhead moving?"

"A hundred and fifty when I was in the hitting area," he gestured with his good hand, making a hitting motion. "But it was going faster afterward—a hundred and fifty-five miles per hour."

"Faster?"

"It has to be faster," he said impatiently. "Otherwise you're not accelerating the clubhead!"

It was exchanges such as this that made me realize how deep Mike's knowledge was of the golf swing. I had once read a book on the physics of the golf swing. It was dense going, filled with complicated formulas and equations to compute flight trajectories and ball spin rates. But one thing I remember well was that if a golfer swings a club at a constant rate, say ninety-nine miles per hour, the ball will travel a certain distance. But if a person is accelerating a club from ninety-nine to one hundred miles per hour at the moment of impact, the ball will go significantly farther. It had to do with the transfer of energy. And since golf is a "dead ball sport" (a sport in which the ball is stationary, not rebounding like in tennis and base-ball), the golfer has to generate all the energy when striking the ball. Mike knew this and achieved his highest speed *after* impact.

We pulled the BMW close to the entrance of the restaurant and Danny helped Mike walk in. I carefully parked the $125,000 car and hurried in to join them. We sat in a booth while the wait-ress brought us drinks. Then, Mike asked Danny to fix a plate of food for him from the buffet. I left my seat to get food for myself, and Danny and I had a chance to talk privately.

"He can be a pain in the butt sometimes," Danny said. "But I dearly love the man."

We took our plates, heaped with food, back to the booth and rejoined Mike. Danny told me stories about what it was like to caddy for him. He described a 2-iron Mike had hit in a tour-nament that sailed 260 yards and caught the lip of a trap by just inches. Otherwise, he would have been on the green and putting for eagle. In the trap the ball plugged and he bogeyed the hole.

"Mike always went for it," Danny said.

"Gene Sarazen—you've heard of him?" Mike asked me.

"Sure. He was one of the best golfers in the thirties."

"Sarazen was one of my best friends on the tour," Mike said.

"He was so impressed with my game that he wanted to quit the tour and manage me. He said he would make a fortune. But after he saw me play he backed out, because he didn't like the way I always tried to make every shot—even if it was a low-odds shot."

One of the stories Danny told that day really stuck with me. He said that Mike was stronger than anyone he'd ever met. He was, as the saying goes, "so strong he didn't know his own strength."

"Once, Mike came over to my place and asked to borrow a torque wrench," Danny said. "I figured he was going to torque down the lug nuts on that old Caddy of his. But I looked out the window and saw he was tightening the head bolts on a VW engine that was lying on the ground that he had lifted out of the trunk of his car. I ran out there with a buddy of mine and said, 'Jeez, Mike, you shouldn't have lifted this by yourself.' I mean, he was about seventy years old at the time. Well, I was working construction at that time, and I was pretty strong. So me and a buddy tried to lift the engine back into the trunk for him. Well, we got it up and set it on the lip of the trunk. But we couldn't lift it high enough to get it in. Mike was watching us, and he just suddenly said, 'Give me that thing,' and he picked it up by himself, held it out at arm's length, and set it in the trunk. That might give you some idea of the strength he had."

We drove back to Mike's house and settled in to wait for

Mike Dunaway. I always liked looking at the sequence shots of Mike's swing that were hanging on the walls. Today, I noticed there was a swing sequence I had never seen before.

"A friend of mine sent me that the other day," Mike said, seeing what I was looking at.

"What are these lines that are drawn on the picture?" I asked. In each frame, straight lines were drawn framing Mike's head and the angle of his torso bending forward from his hips.

"Those pictures were taken at an event I attended in nineteen seventy-five in Kansas City," Mike said. "A bunch of golf equipment manufacturers sponsored it and got all the golfers together to find out who had the best swing. They had us all swing and took pictures of the positions we were in. Then the sports writers voted on who had the best swing."

I was beginning to sense where this was going. "Okay, so who had the best swing?"

"They chose mine," Mike said. "So I have two of the highest achievements you can get in golf—the longest drive and the greatest golf swing."

I looked at the pictures once more, studying each frame and the position it showed. There it was for anyone to see: the greatest golf swing. Of all the people who were playing the game at that time, Mike's swing was the best. Seeing Mike frozen in the different stages of the swing made it look so effortless, as if I could just assume those positions and get the same result. The proof of how superior this swing was could be found in how quickly Dunaway and others had improved their game under Mike's teaching. Under Danny's watchful eye, and Mike's tutelage, I hoped to soon be the latest success story for the Austin swing.

We heard the front door open, and a voice cheerfully called out, "Michael?"

Mike sat up straight in his chair. "Yes sir! Come in. Come in."

Mike Dunaway appeared around the edge of the hallway. I had seen him before in the video *Mike Austin: Secrets from the Game's Longest Hitter,* but since then he had lost a lot of weight. He was a good-looking guy with a head of thick brown hair and a deep tan. He shook my hand and greeted us all. Mike Austin was beaming with happiness to see Dunaway.

"Where's that machine you've been telling me about?" Mike asked eagerly.

"In my car," Dunaway said. "Can I set it up in here?"

"Hell, yes. We want to see what all the commotion is about."

We helped Dunaway bring in the components of the swing trainer and assembled it in the living room across from Mike's Barcalounger. It was basically a board with an upright pole from which an arm suspended a golf grip. The golfer stood on the board and swung the grip as if it were a golf club. The purpose of the contraption was both to provide exercise and to groove the right swing motions.

Dunaway stood on the board, took the grip, and demonstrated it vigorously as he made the Austin "compound pivot."

After learning Mike Austin's swing, Mike Dunaway won the top U.S. and world driving contests.

Danny got on the board next and tried it out. I looked over and saw Mike's eyes studying his movements closely.

"Want to give it a whirl?" Dunaway asked me in his Arkansas twang.

I took my position and held the grip. But as soon as I moved, I heard the familiar explosion from Mike. "The shoulder goes down! It never goes out!"

"He's trying to turn," Dunaway said to Danny. His tone was pitying, as if someone referring to a sinner who hasn't yet been saved. "Bend the left leg and move the hips sideways."

I tried to do what he said.

"No, sir!" Mike yelled. "You'll lose all your power that way, and your head will sway. Let the shoulder come under the— NOT THAT WAY!"

Danny stepped in. "Mike, I'll get him straightened out and then you can look him over, see what you think."

Boy, was I looking forward to those lessons. I wanted to be able to stand in front of Mike with confidence and make a golf swing without him taking my head off.

"Can I ask you to look at some video?" Dunaway asked Mike.

Mike nodded, looking pleased. Dunaway pulled out a small video camera and connected it with a cable to the large-screen TV in front of Mike. He turned it on and we saw pictures of him hitting balls with a driver. After each shot he watched the ball and said, "Three-forty, ten yards right . . ." "Three-twenty, dead straight . . ." Apparently, he was

"He has unlimited power and
an excellent knowledge of the
golf swing."

Mike Austin

*Mike Dunaway demonstrates the action of the
compound pivot.*

describing the distance he hit the ball and the amount off line it was.

"The thing I'm having trouble with is the hand motion at the top of the backswing," Dunaway said. "It still feels herky-jerky to me."

They slowed the camera down so it moved frame by frame. It was a good way to analyze the motions of the backswing. Unfortunately, the downswing was so fast that the club was virtually invisible.

"You're not in the correct position at the top of the backswing," Mike told him.

"But when I do what you tell me to do, it doesn't feel right," Dunaway replied. "Look here, I get to this point"– he pointed at himself on the TV screen–"and when I try to take it back from there I lose the position."

They began to discuss the nuances of one small section of the swing in a way that I couldn't completely follow. Their disagreement seemed to center on how much the wrist should be cocked. Mike wanted Dunaway to have his hand in the "broken wrist" position rather than in a neutral position. As the discussion continued, the volume of their voices began to rise.

"I don't see why the heck I need to do that," Dunaway said. "I mean, I'm hitting the ball three hundred forty yards on the carry and dead straight as it is."

Mike countered that there was still more distance to be gained if he improved his hand position.

It was amazing for me to be in the room with two men who

were arguing about being able to routinely hit the ball over 340 yards. However, I had to remind myself that Mike had hit it significantly farther than Dunaway, and he did it at the age of sixty-four without today's advanced clubs.

The voices of the two men continued to rise in volume until they were shouting at the top of their lungs. At one point I remember Danny trying to make the peace by saying, "Jesus, Mike, calm down or you'll have another stroke."

They ignored him. As the two men came to loggerheads and Mike could think of no other way to argue his point, he suddenly shook his finger at Dunaway and bellowed, "You can't go against God! You can't go against God!" Even in the midst of this furious battle of words, I had to smile at Mike's assertion and its implication. He seemed to be saying that his swing was divinely ordained—perfect and beyond criticism. I even pictured the testimonial that could be put on Mike's next golf instructional video: "This is by far the best swing"—Almighty God.

Danny became so tired of this shouting match that he announced he was leaving. I also seized this opportunity to escape and followed him out the door. Mike and Dunaway didn't seem to notice us leave. We could still hear the intense discussion even after we closed the door. We stood outside beside our cars, in the stifling heat, and talked for a few minutes.

"I have to tell you something about Mike," Danny said. "He comes from an era where he doesn't believe in giving everything away."

"What do you mean?"

"When you go to him for a lesson, he helps you out, and he gives you a little of this and a little of that. But I think he always holds a little something back. I think all teachers do that."

I was astounded—and yet it made sense now that Danny brought it to my attention. "You mean that Mike has never revealed the full secret to anyone? Even to Mike Dunaway?"

"Remember, he's probably the longest hitter that's ever lived. So maybe there's something he's held back all his life," Danny said. "But I'll tell you one thing, I think I've figured it out. And I'm putting all that in this book," he said, tapping his laptop, which held his manuscript.

"But can it be explained so that the average golfer will be able to do it?" I asked.

That question gave him pause. He squinted and thought it over carefully. "They're not going to hit the ball like Mike Austin, I'll tell you that much. He was phenomenally strong and he had incredible timing. But if the average golfer understands the swing, and commits to taking the time to change his game—and we're talkin' months, not weeks—he'll hit the ball much longer and much, much straighter. Once you get this swing dialed in, the ball goes where you aim it."

That was enough for me. "Okay. When can we get together at the range? I want you to look at what I've got and straighten me out."

We compared dates and agreed to meet several weeks later, when I returned from my family vacation in Virginia. As I got in the car, I could still hear loud voices coming from the house.

The next day Mike called me and apologized for the episode.

"That's okay," I said. "I know how passionate you are about these things."

"I had to straighten him out," Mike said. "He called me this morning and told me he's got it now. He said he's killin' the ball."

That was Mike's point of view. But I couldn't help wondering what Dunaway thought. As a journalist I knew it was important to hear as many sides of the story as possible before deciding about the truth of the matter. This was what I was about to do while in Virginia, even though I hadn't yet told Mike my plans. As I would soon find out, I was about to take the last step in fully believing the power of the Austin swing.

CHAPTER 14

CHANDLER HARPER

In my career as a journalist, I've found that I tend to overlook one important part of every story I'm working on. In this case my oversight was that I never tried to reach Chandler Harper, who had been playing in the tournament with Mike in Las Vegas when Mike hit his world-record drive. My fatal assumption had been that Harper was no longer living. Or if he was, that he was unreachable. Assumptions are dangerous for a journalist. And as it turned out, neither assumption was correct.

This overlooked part of the Mike Austin story came to mind when I realized my family's vacation in Virginia would take us close to where Harper lived. Early on, I had toyed with the idea of trying to call Harper to verify Mike's long drive. In fact, I had asked Mike for his phone number. Mike shuffled through his tattered Rolodex, looking for a number. Finally, he gave up, saying, "I think he's at a golf course somewhere in Virginia called the Bide-A-Wee. Maybe you can get it through information." Trying several different spellings and doing a statewide search, I finally found the Bide-A-Wee in Portsmouth, Virginia.

I convinced the starter in the pro shop to get Chandler Harper's number. I hesitantly asked if Mr. Harper was still in good health. "Oh, yes," the starter said. "He's out here at the course a couple of times a week. And he still plays golf."

I really had only one question I wanted to ask Chandler Harper. I could have easily covered it in a few minutes on the phone. But the more I thought about Harper, the more I thought this would be a good opportunity to meet another golf legend. After all, he had won eight PGA tournaments, including the 1950 PGA Championship. He also appeared in the first televised golf match, the 1953 World Championship at Tam O'Shanter in Chicago, where fellow Virginian Lew Worsham holed a 104-yard shot from the fairway for an eagle 2 and a one-shot victory.

I telephoned Harper and explained that I was writing a book about Mike Austin, then asked if he would meet me at the Bide-A-Wee to talk about Mike's record-setting drive. He recalled Mike immediately and said he would be happy to meet with me and provide whatever details he could.

My brother-in-law, Brad Swingle, who lives in Richmond, is an avid golfer, so I asked him to accompany me to the Bide-A-Wee. He told me that growing up in Virginia he had often heard about Harper and would be honored to sit in on the interview. We arrived fifteen minutes early and, walking into the clubhouse, saw a portrait of Harper in his prime, sharply handsome and looking very sporty in a cardigan and a jaunty straw hat. A plaque under his picture listed the major tournaments he had won.

Looking into the snack shop, we saw the man from the portrait, now eighty-nine years old. Harper was carefully dressed, in a checked sports coat, a striped shirt, white pants, and a porkpie hat with "Bide-A-Wee" embossed on the crown. As I approached him, he turned sharp eyes on me and thrust his hand out. His grip was still strong and his eyes were bright under hooded lids. I felt I was in the presence of a proud, intelligent Southern gentleman. It was only later that he sadly acknowledged how his golfing ability had diminished drastically in the past few years. "I'm weak as a kitten now," he said.

I introduced Harper to my brother-in-law and they chatted about different golf courses in Virginia. The three of us took a seat on a veranda looking out on the first and tenth holes of the Bide-A-Wee, a course Harper designed and managed, which had opened in 1956. It was an overcast day and, thankfully, not muggy-hot the way most summer days are in Virginia. As we talked, a nearby air conditioner clicked on and off. Occasionally the starter's voice would come over a loudspeaker calling golfers to the first tee. While Harper spun stories of the past, I saw the lean old fingers of his right hand drumming lightly on the back of his left hand. I thought of the nickname other players on the tour had given Harper: "Old Sawbones."

Chandler seemed ready for me to launch into my questions about Mike Austin and his long drive. But I set those questions aside initially. I told him I was honored to be spending some time with him and wanted to know more about his life and golfing career.

Chandler Harper had taken up golf at the age of nine, playing on the courses in the same area of Portsmouth, Virginia, where we now sat. He loved the game immediately and began winning tournaments at an early age. He was self-taught, modeling his swing after photos and newsreel clips he saw of Bobby Jones. Sometime later, as a fifteen-year-old, he sought out Jones and met him coming out of the locker room after a local tournament.

"Mr. Jones," Chandler told the great champion, "I've been patterning my swing after yours for several years now. I'm particularly interested in your chipping. Would you mind explaining to me how you go about it?"

Jones looked at this young, earnest, ambitious golfer and said, "Son, let's sit down a moment and talk." They took a seat on a nearby bench and Jones began his explanation of the art of chipping. "The important thing is not to get wedded to any one club, because the conditions change all the time. In some cases you'll need to chip with a spoon. In other cases you need to use a long iron and let it run thirty feet to the hole. Use whatever club you need to get it on the green, then let it roll out from there. And another thing, never backspin the ball unless you have to, unless there's a reason for it."

I thought how interesting it was that both Austin and Harper had crossed paths with Bobby Jones. Although he was long dead, Jones's words—and his advice—were coming to me now only once removed. I felt close to history thinking of Jones, in the prime of life, giving advice to the young golfer.

I asked Harper, "Did Jones's advice help you?"

"I stuck to it all my life," he said. "I think I was one of the best chippers out there. I got credit for being a great putter too. I couldn't have won anything otherwise. You had to chip and putt to win."

"Okay, then," I said. "So what's the secret to putting?"

"I always thought the secret to good putting was getting the putter straight back," he said, making a putting stroke with his old hands. "Don't let the blade get outside. When I got into a habit of doing that, I missed the putt on the left side."

"You pull the putt slightly."

"Well, if you start the club on the outside, your putter's gonna be traveling that direction so you'll miss left. I think the thing is, if you learn to take the thing straight back you'll get an even stroke. Make the length of the stroke according to how far you're gonna putt it. The other thing I did was just take one good look at the putt. Then, I'd walk up and stroke the ball. I figured my first look would be my truest."

We talked for quite awhile about Ben Hogan, whom Harper had played with many times on the tour. I had to ask him what it was like to play with him.

"When he got on the first tee, it was all business with him,"

Harper said. "He wasn't real popular. One time, I remember Jimmy Demaret came into a hotel and saw Hogan sitting by himself. He said, 'Well, there's Ben Hogan and all his friends.' But Snead was a big favorite with the galleries. He was kind of loose, telling jokes all the time."

"Was Hogan the greatest player from that era?" I asked.

"People ask me frequently who was the best. I can name them right off: Hogan, Snead, and Byron Nelson—in that order."

"What made Hogan so great?"

"He was absolutely determined to be good. He got a terrible start, his father committed suicide in front of him when he was nine years old. But he was determined to be good. He had the goods that you've got to have to be great. He had a strong will and he would never let anything stop him."

Yes, I thought. I know that quality in a person. You can sense it in everything they do. No wonder a mystique had grown up around Hogan that made him such a presence in golf even today.

It was fortunate that I had brought my brother-in-law with me, because although Harper looked at me when I asked a question, he always delivered his answer to Brad. I think he felt more comfortable talking to another Southerner, and to someone who was such a great fan. Brad smiled and nodded in reaction to everything Harper said. Then, when Harper was done answering, he would turn back to me for the next question.

Finally, I sensed that Harper was warmed up, so I decided to get down to business.

"I know you didn't know Mike Austin very well," I said, "but I want to pick your brains a little bit about him. Had you ever heard of Mike before that tournament?"

"No. I had not," he answered. "But Mike was quite a fella. He wrote a poem that one night and gave it to my wife."

"I know he's something of a poet on top of everything else. When you played with him, what did you think of his swing?" I asked. "Was it any different than the other players'?"

"He's the longest driver I've ever seen. And he didn't look like he was hitting it too hard. I've seen long hitters who hit it hard, but Mike took his time taking the club back, then came through the ball real smooth."

I tried to picture Mike Austin back in 1974, meeting Harper at the tournament in Las Vegas. Mike was already sixty-four years old then. What was he like?

"Did you have any kind of a feeling about what Mike was like as a person?" I asked Harper. "Did you like him or dislike him?"

"Yes, I liked him," he said in a way that I really couldn't read. "He was very funny. We would see him at the inn at night. We wouldn't eat with him, but we'd see him and talk to him. He'd come over and talk to my wife a couple times. He liked her, he wrote a poem for her. I forgot what it was about, but he wrote it."

Now I was ready to move on to the more controversial material. I was careful of the way I phrased my questions.

"I wanted to ask you about that day when Mike hit that record-setting drive. Can you describe what happened?"

Wednesday, September 15, 1971

The Flint Journal

Golfer Mike Austin Makes Boasts... Then Backs Them Up

By BRUCE JOHNS

Mike Austin is a man of many talents and takes pride in backing them up.

He says he can out-drive any member of the Michigan Section PGA and won't hesitate to prove it. Boom ... 300 yards! Boom ... 300 yards! Drives soar during an exhibition for a few doubtful onlookers.

AFTER SHOWING his muscle to hit a ball conventionally, Austin will take swipes one-handed — either hand — and still knock it 200 yards. He'll move over to the left side, turn the club face upside down and hit a shot many amateurs would cherish.

The Chenuego Hills' pro claims he has sung opera and will rip off a few bars of Granada to erase any doubt. Maybe Flint Journal music critic Ed Hayman wouldn't reward the mustachioed golfer and A plus for his singing ability, but Austin did present a pleasant, soothing voice.

"I've done many things," said Austin, a world traveler who was born on the isle of Guernsey off Great Britain.

HIS MOST remarkable claim is the study of kinesiology, the research of muscular motion for the manipulation of all joints.

"In other words it helps

Decatur, Ga. "That means No. 1 hitter.

"THERE'S A machine that records the impact of how hard a guy hits the ball. Jack Nicklaus scored 116 with a 11-ounce club, George Baird had 115 with a 13½ ounce club and Chi Chi Rodriquez had 110 with a 13 ounce club. I had 127 with a 15 ounce club.

"In fact, I was playing in a tournament in Stockton, Calif., and Chi Chi was in front of us. His group was three holes behind and he was playing real slow. So, I kept hitting into them, trying to hit Chi Chi with my drives after he hit his second shot. I ran him off the course on the 13th hole."

AUSTIN, WHO is married to Tanya Somva, a Russian girl in show business, said he played the professional tour off and on over the years.

"My best finish was eighth in the Crosby Open in 1953. I had a chance to win the Tucson Open in 1957 but four-putted the last hole. I was putting for an eagle from eight feet, knocked it eight feet past the hole and missed a two-footer."

"This guy hits the ball a ton," said John Chester, pro at Davison.

Added Sal Pomante, tournament director for the PGA: "He can hit it further than

use from six different joints at the time of impact."

AUSTIN SAID the secret to retaining one's muscle tone in correct breathing, eating habits and posture.

"You should also give up smoking and drinking. When I was studying the disection of the human body during my internship at Emory, I saw the lung of a smoker and the lung

quit after you see the difference.

"Drinking affects the liver," said Austin, while sipping his beer.

After the conversation, other reliable sources were asked if Austin was a phoney. As far as anyone knew, everything he said was true.

Muscular Mike should add one more distinction to his

—Journal Photo by WILLIAM M. GALLAGHER

Mike Austin ... Man of Many Talents, Distinctions

Sometimes Mike's feats were hard to believe.

Harper took a deep breath and drummed his fingers on the back of his other hand. He seemed to be looking back in time and imagining the event.

"The hole was about four hundred and fifty yards long," he began. "Mike hit his drive, and it went a mile high up in the air. We saw it take off, and we knew it was a long one. But when we got to our balls, we all had at least a hundred-yard second shot. Well, we couldn't find Mike's ball anywhere. I happened to look beyond the green on the next tee, and it looked like a white ball there. I said, 'Mike, this is impossible, but why don't you go over there and look at that ball and see if it's yours.' Right off he described his ball; he said, 'I was hitting Titleist,' and I think he gave us a number, I think he said number one. They ran over there and they found that the ball was his—nobody else's—it was the one he had just hit off the tee. A few days later I got a call from London from the *Guinness* people. They said, 'I understand you were playing with Mike Austin. We've got some figures we want to verify with you.' Whatever I told them almost matched what they had. They said, 'Well, that's good enough for us. We're going to regard that as the world's longest drive.'"

"I understand that hole is level," I said. "But was it windy?" I had to ask this, because I knew every golfer would be looking for a way to explain away this great drive.

"Well, when we were on the green, the flag started to flap around and we all joked that the wind had come down off this big mountain that was behind us. But, no, it wasn't especially windy."

It was time to ask the question that had brought me there. It was the only real question I had wanted to ask Harper, but I wanted to make sure it was introduced at the right moment. It was the question I had had in my mind since I had met Mike and heard about his accomplishment.

"When I tell people that Mike Austin hit a drive five hundred and fifteen yards, they say that's impossible, you can't hit a ball that far," I said. I continued carefully. "Do you have any doubt that that was his ball, that he did hit it that far?"

Harper didn't blink, or look away, or give any signs of eva-siveness. He quickly said, "No, I don't have any doubt about it at all. It could have been off by a yard or two, but we stepped it off and took big steps back to the center of the green."

There it was, confirmation from one of the great golfers of the past century, Chandler Harper, an expert in his field who knew what was possible and what was impossible. And he said that Mike had done what he claimed to have done: hit a golf ball 515 yards in a tournament. I felt myself relaxing, laying down my suspicions for the last time. My job as a journalist— as a professional skeptic—was over. I had verified the record as much as I could without finding a time machine and literally going back to 1974.

Brad and I chatted with Harper for a few more minutes as we went outside and stood in front of the clubhouse. As we talked, a car slid up behind us, the engine idling softly. An African-American woman was sitting behind the steering wheel patiently waiting.

"Here's my housekeeper," Harper said. "I don't know what I'd do without her."

PGA Pro Chandler Harper witnessed Mike's record drive.

We shook hands and said good-bye. He climbed into the big car and rode off.

As I drove back to our vacation house, I felt relieved. Whatever doubt had been in my mind about Mike and his claims was slipping away now. A new thought began to take its place: What if Mike Austin was not only strong and athletic, but what if he really had created a golf swing that was vastly superior than what is currently being used and taught? After all, size, strength, athleticism, and the dry Nevada air might account for a gain of 50 yards. But Mike had hit his drive at the age of sixty-four using a persimmon-headed driver with a steel shaft, and he was still 100 yards longer than today's biggest hitters.

If Mike's swing was superior, why hadn't anyone else learned the secret? Mike's demanding personality probably had kept most people at a distance from him. Those who had penetrated his crusty exterior had shown incredible improvement. Mike Dunaway, for one, had learned the Austin swing in about six months and captured a national long-drive contest—and then a world long-drive tournament. Danny had told me about a young guy, Jaacob Bowden, whom he had been teaching. He had learned the swing in five months and was now winning long-drive contests with drives of 380 yards.

Watching the Virginia countryside rolling by, I thought of my own 300-yard goal. It had been awhile since I had made progress toward that milestone. Maybe Danny Shauger could help me decode the dense tangle of tips and information I had received from Mike over the past few years and help me join the ranks of the big hitters.

CHAPTER 15

TIN CUP TEACHER

The San Fernando Valley, north of Los Angeles, sprawls in every direction until it hits the surrounding barren mountains. "The Valley," as Los Angelenos call it, is sealed off from the ocean breezes that keep the rest of the urban area cool. As a result, temperatures in the summer often soar over a hundred. This area was rapidly developed after World War II and is filled with fifties-style diners, bowling alleys, and mile after mile of tract homes. In the far corner of the Valley is the John Wells Driving Range, an open city block where golfers hit out toward flags stuck into the artificial turf that covers the ground. This is where I met Danny Shauger one hot summer morning for my first lesson.

"I'm Tin Cup," Danny told me at one point during our lesson, likening himself to the Kevin Costner character in the 1996 movie seen by virtually every golfer on the planet. I thought this was an apt comparison for a student of Mike Austin since Tin Cup's failing was his stubborn insistence on always "going for it"—trying to hit the ball on the green from impossible distances. Still, I was interested to hear why Danny had made this comparison.

"Really? What makes you Tin Cup?" I asked.

"Well, I live in a trailer, I drive an old car, I don't have a lot of money, and I love golf," he said. "I'm Tin Cup. But I do have my golf book. And when people realize that I've put the essence of the Mike Austin swing down on paper, they're going to buy my book. What I've got is worth one hell of a lot of money."

It was a variation on the Hollywood dream that said, "Don't pay attention to where I'm living today and what I'm driving today, because sometime in the future I'm going to make it big."

"Yes, well, I've been reading your book," I said. "And it's very good. But how much do you think people can learn about the golf swing from a book?"

"Look at Hogan's book, *Five Lessons: The Modern Fundamentals of Golf.* There isn't a golfer who picks up a club who doesn't know that book inside and out. Now, I've got something more valuable than Hogan. I've got the secret from the man who hit the ball better than anyone, ever. What do you think that will be worth?"

I had to admit he was right. That was why I was here, on this driving range, on this hot Tuesday morning. I was trying to learn the secret to a superior swing, a swing that was demonstrated so dramatically throughout Mike Austin's life. Over the past several weeks I had been reading the manuscript, written by Danny with Mike's input, which was at that time titled *The*

Formula for Power and Accuracy (and eventually self-published under the title *Kill the Ball*). The book was rough around the edges, but it was filled with things about the golf swing I had never heard explained before. And by this time, I had read just about every golf book on the market. Danny's manuscript took many of the things Mike told me in cryptic nuggets and explained them in detail. The problem was that to reach mainstream popularity the book would need a level of polish that it didn't yet have.

"By the way," I said, "I've been making some edits. Let me give it to you." I reached into my golf bag for the manuscript, but he stopped me.

"Hang on to it," he said. "I've changed everything around since I saw you last."

"What should I do with it?" I asked.

"Hang on to it for now. Okay, let's get started with the lesson."

Danny pulled a club from my bag and laid it on the driving range mat to represent the ball's line of flight. He then asked me to take out my sand wedge and grip the club. He adjusted my grip somewhat, since Austin recommends a slightly different way of holding the club that allows a fuller release. Then, Danny showed me how if you take the club back so that the wrists turn the opposite way than the PGA swing, the path of the club will go on a straight line. To illustrate this, he had me line up with the clubhead poised above the shaft of the club lying on the mat. As I took the club back, I could see that it was moving in a straight line along the shaft of the club lying on the mat.

"I call this 'the little swing inside the big swing,'" Danny said. "If you keep the wrists loose so that that the club makes this motion as you come down into the ball, the ball will go straight. What gives the swing the power is the pivot and turn of the shoulders. So if you take this small swing and add the Austin pivot and shoulder turn, you have the Austin golf swing."

Bells went off in my head. Wow, I actually understood that! Not only that, but it lined up perfectly with what Mike had told me all along.

Danny had me hit some chip shots with just my hands. The action broke all the rules of golf commonly taught, since it felt like a scooping action. Teaching pros tell golfers this is a major sin, that the wrists should be locked when they come through the ball. If they aren't locked, teachers say, the wrists have "broken down." However, using this new wrist action I was able to hit the ball straighter than ever before. Not only that, but the click of the ball was sweet music to my ears. It was crisp and true, showing me that I was making good contact.

"Once you get this action," Danny told me. "You'll start chipping in a lot. You line it up, chip the ball, and it goes where you aim. It's amazing."

"But it's a scooping motion, and most teachers are totally against that."

"It sure is different. But as you see, it works. Once you use this motion in the full swing, you'll find that you're hitting your ball higher with more backspin. The ball flies farther and checks up when it hits the green. Those are all good things. So who cares what the other teachers say? Like Sam Snead said, 'It's not a game of how, it's a game of how many.'"

For the rest of the lesson, Danny had me working on the Austin pivot. This was the motion I had done incorrectly at Mike's house when Dunaway was there. With Danny's supervision, and his patience, I was able to begin to feel the pivot I had seen Mike demonstrate in his videos. It really wasn't that difficult, but I kept finding myself wanting to turn my hips rather than to tilt them up and down.

Once I had the pivot, Danny said I needed to work on getting all the way to the top of the backswing. To help me do this he caught my left arm as I took it back. I was ready to stop my backswing, but he said, "Bring it back . . . back . . . back . . . A little more." His voice was soft, almost seductive, as if to say, "Try something new and dangerous—you'll love it." I felt myself arriving in a strange new position. Of course it felt awkward, because it was so new to me. But it also felt powerful. I believed that from here, if I connected, the ball would really take off.

Danny shifted his grip to my hands. "Now, the downswing starts with a light toss of the club that feels like this." He moved my hands in the right direction. "Just a light toss that I call 'spinning the meatballs off the plate.'"

I had been holding this position for a long time, and when I heard his "spinning the meatballs off the plate," I couldn't hold my position any longer. I relaxed, laughing. "Do you really call it that?"

"Mike calls it a 'back throw,' because it's like tossing the club behind you. But I like to call it 'spinning the meatballs off the plate.' Your right hand is in the position of a waiter holding a tray. If you make a light toss of the club, coupled with the shift, you will arrive in this position with the club perfectly square and moving at a very high rate of speed."

Danny illustrated the toss and the impact position. He froze his position at impact, and I saw he was in a position I had seen Mike assume in many stop-action photos. The weight of his hips and much of his upper body had swung past the ball, but his clubhead was just reaching the ball. "This is a terrifically powerful impact position," Danny said. "When you learn to hit the ball from this position, you'll get a feeling you've never had before."

I thought back to my first meeting with Mike and his story about his earliest golf lesson. The pro had told him to bury the head of the club in the wet bank without getting any mud on his sleeve. The throwing motion that Danny was now describing seemed a copy of what Mike had learned in the exercise he was taught as a child.

For the rest of the lesson, Danny had me hitting sand wedges while making this aggressive weight shift. It was discouraging,

*Danny Shauger demonstrates the throwing motion in the
Mike Austin swing.*

because for about twenty balls I just couldn't get it at all. My
club was way out in front of my weight shift.

Danny stopped my efforts and suddenly said, "Shake
my hand."

I obeyed. He took my hand and held on to it.

"Now, you're a writer and I'm a golf pro. But who has smoother hands?"

I suddenly felt a little embarrassed. My hands felt like sandpaper against his smooth skin.

"Your hands are like a stone mason's! You know why? Because you're working too hard. Lighten your grip and relax. Now try it again."

I addressed the ball and tried again. Several balls later I felt a sensation I'd never experienced before. It came later in the swing, and the contact was so solid it was—paradoxically—almost silent. It felt as though the last tumbler in a bank vault had just slid into place and the door was finally swinging open. It was a feeling that came up through my arms and glowed in my body.

"There it is!" Danny said. "You just did it!"

Naturally, when I tried to do it again I was unsuccessful. But since I had done it once, I knew I would eventually learn it. At least now I had a clear road map of things I needed to work on.

I thanked Danny for the lesson and invited him to send me the latest installment of his instructional book so I could edit and critique it. As I drove home I reviewed what I had learned. I was eager to talk to Mike to confirm some of the points Danny had taught me. But, unfortunately, my full-time job monopolized my time for the rest of the week. I postponed my trip to see Mike until the weekend. Late Friday afternoon, I got a message from Danny. His voice on my answering machine was subdued.

"When you called I was in the hospital," he said.

"What's wrong?"

"This morning I went over to visit Mike, and I found him lying on the floor. He had fallen and broken his hip. They're operating on him tonight, but the doctor tells me he might not survive the operation." He sighed and spoke in a tone of voice I'd never heard before. "I'm afraid we're going to lose him."

I thanked Danny for letting me know and promised to call him to find out how the operation went. Before I hung up he said, "I just hope I can get my book into print before he goes. I want him to know I got it all down on paper. It's my gift to him." I knew the feeling myself. I was anxious to get Mike's memoir, which was still circulating among publishing houses, into print while Mike had time to enjoy the recognition it gave him.

That night, at home with my family, I thought of Mike in the hospital, undergoing surgery. I remembered how my grandfather had broken his hip and then died only a few days later. I felt there was a good chance Mike would pass away during the night. The next morning I called Danny, who was at the hospital visiting Mike.

"He pulled through okay," Danny said. "But he's in a hell of a lot of pain. Here's his phone number in his room. I know it would mean a lot to him if you called."

I dialed his number, not knowing what to expect. It rang several times and was then answered. A voice spoke, but the words were garbled. I could barely make out his voice saying, "Mike Austin." It was a distant memory of his previously strong voice. But he did answer the phone. I took that to mean that he wasn't ready to go.

"I wanted you to know that I'm thinking of you, Mike," I said.

He answered, but I couldn't understand what he said. I didn't know what to do. So I told him that I had been taking lessons from Danny and that I was hitting the ball better than ever. I said I was coming closer to understand the beauty of the thing he had invented: the Austin swing. When I was done, his whispering voice spoke again, but I still couldn't hear what he said.

"Okay, Mike, I better let you rest. I'll come to see you soon."

I hung up feeling terrible. I felt awful for Mike, in such pain that he couldn't even speak intelligibly. But I was also sobered by the vision of what I would probably face someday. Right now, I was perfectly healthy, with years of golf still to be played; hopefully, I still had my best golf in front of me. Someday, though, my days would run out too. I would be in a hospital bed with only a phone to connect me to the rest of the world. Would I want to continue living as much as Mike did? I sure hoped so, because besides life—and golf—what is there?

Over the next month I had two more lessons from Danny at the John Wells Driving Range. We always began by talking about Mike's condition, then discussing Danny's book. He still felt he was in a race to get the book into print while Mike was still with us. The problem was that he was finding so much to say. He was taking virtually a lifetime of teaching from Mike and trying to get it between the covers of a book. My efforts to edit the book were always accepted and my ideas were welcome, but the manuscript kept changing faster than I could edit it.

It was during these lessons with Danny that I began the most significant changes to my swing. The reverse action of the hands in the Austin swing at times seemed too great a change. But I knew through my free throw shooting research that it takes at least twenty-eight days to bring a significant change to an athletic motion. I was committing to the changes and keeping faith that at some point in the future the changes would bring rewards. There were flashes of improvement, including the time when I hit a 7-iron that climbed into the flat sky of the San Fernando Valley and didn't seem to want to come down. Danny watched it approvingly. "That's a hundred and seventy-yard seven-iron!" he said, sharing my success.

My swing had changed so much that I didn't dare take it onto the golf course. However, the first round I played I shot in the mid-80s—my usual score. So, at least I hadn't lost ground. On the plus side, I chipped in for a birdie and left many of my chips so close they were easy tap-in putts.

In late September, Mike was released from the hospital. When he got home and was settling in, lying in a bed in the living room, Danny walked in and found himself standing in two inches of water. A pipe had burst under the house. As Mike lay there recovering, plumbers and contractors waded through the water, trying to find the break in the pipe. Hearing all this, I said it was a wonder that Mike didn't just give up and decide that living wasn't worth the hassle.

"Are you kidding me?" Danny said. "He's having the time of his life. He's talking with all the workers and giving them golf lessons from his bed. I told him, 'Mike, you're amazing. I don't know how you keep going. If I were you, the bad part of me would have killed the good part by now.' "

Mike didn't stay at home long. He seemed to go downhill quickly, and one day when Danny took him in for a blood test, he passed out in the car. They took him back into the hospital, and once again the prognosis wasn't good. Danny worked feverishly on the book, trying to get it into print so his friend and teacher could see it.

I was working on a similar deadline, trying to sell the memoir about Mike. The more deeply I came to know Mike, and the more I grew to like and admire him, the more puzzled and frustrated I became that he never got the recognition he deserved. When the *Times* article appeared Mike had gotten one brief day in the sun. But that story only scratched the surface. My book, I hoped, would more fully chronicle his amazing life and finally place him in the history books where he belonged, along with the other golf heroes of his time.

CHAPTER 16

THE LIVING AUSTIN SWING

Whenever I visited Mike in the hospital, he mentioned Jaacob Bowden, who had learned the Austin swing from Danny and was using it to win long-drive contests across the country. Danny said he had run into Jaacob at a driving range and, when he heard Danny was a teacher, asked him to take a look at his swing, since he wanted to qualify for the PGA tour.

Danny watched Jaacob hit some balls and then leveled this verdict: "Ain't no way you're gonna make it on the tour with that swing." However, he added, "I'd like to work with you and teach you a better way of hitting the ball. It was developed by Mike Austin, who is in the *Guinness Book of World Records* for hitting the longest drive in competition. If you fully learn the Austin swing, you'll have all the distance and accuracy you'll need to qualify for the tour."

For the next six months, Danny worked with Jaacob almost every day, the way Mike had worked with Dunaway some years previously. At first his progress was slow and his scores shot up. But his scores quickly dropped to where they had been—

and then began going lower and lower. As promised, the length of his drives increased by 100 yards and more. Jaacob decided to head out on the long-drive tour. Surprisingly, there is little overlap between PGA golf tournaments and long-drive events. The contestants on the long-drive circuit exist in a sub-culture with colorful nicknames like Sean "The Beast" Fister. They are bulked-up weight lifters with long-shafted clubs and violent, unorthodox swings. After all, there is only one goal—to have the longest drive that stays in the grid.

Mike had participated in the first world long-drive competition, held at the Tam O'Shanter Golf Course outside Chicago in 1946. He had said that since this was just after World War II, rubber was still in short supply and the balls were dead. If you dropped a ball from the height of your head, it would bounce up only to your knees, while modern balls dropped from this height will bounce up to your chest. To qualify for the event you had to be able to hit the ball over 250 yards. Mike won that competition with three drives that averaged 320 yards. The next closest single drive was 294 yards. Mike won many of these long-drive tournaments and competed in the "350 Club" with Mike Dunaway. Between the ages of seventy-five and seventy-nine, Mike still averaged 312 yards—and he never missed the grid. During his entire career, Mike won forty-eight long-driving contests.

The format at most modern long-drive events is usually the same: Each contestant hits six balls into the grid. The golfer who hits the longest ball that stays in the grid is the winner. In Jaacob's first event, in Phoenix, he placed in the top ten (eighth out of 125 contestants) with a drive of 343 yards. In his sixth event, in St. Louis, at the Pinnacle Distance Challenge, he won with a drive of 381 yards.

After hearing about Jaacob several times, I decided I had to meet him and see his version of the Austin swing with my own eyes. I called Jaacob on his cell phone and learned that he was, at that moment, in Kansas City. He had a plain Midwestern accent and sounded like a thoughtful, unassuming young man. We arranged to meet later that week, when he returned to Southern California. When he pulled up outside my house later that week, I went outside to greet him and found him talking on his cell phone.

"I'm sorry," he said to me, still holding the phone to his ear. "My car was broken into last night and my wallet was stolen. I'm canceling my credit cards."

Later, Jaacob explained that he was living off his savings while trying to qualify for the PGA tour. He had worked as an engineer for about four years in Kansas City and banked all the money he could save—about $40,000. Then he sold all of his things, left all of his friends, and moved to California with nothing more than what he could fit in his car. He lived in a garage in Simi Valley, near Los Angeles, which he rented for $150 a month. While on the road, competing in long-drive events, he slept in his 1997 Toyota

Camry, which had 120,000 miles on it. He had removed the front passenger seat and put in some cushions so he could sleep in it. With a screen across his windshield and tinted windows, no one could see inside. The trunk of Jaacob's car held two sets of golf clubs and the four long-shafted drivers (48 inches long) he used for competition.

"Unlike most guys pursuing golf careers, I don't have a rich family to support me while I do this," he explained. "I have to cut expenses any way I can to stretch my savings. If I sleep in my car, that saves fifty bucks a night. Hopefully, before my own savings run out I'll be able to find a sponsor to help keep me going."

I suggested we go to a driving range in Seal Beach, which was near my house.

"I don't have my wallet, so I can't buy any balls," Jaacob apologized. I told him I'd cover the cost of balls for the pleasure of seeing him hit the long drive. I had learned from his Web site (www.jaacobbowden.com) that Jaacob was six feet, two inches tall and weighed 205 pounds. This was about the height and weight Mike had been in his prime. Jaacob's presence was very different from Mike's, though. He was soft-spoken, deferential, and with that Midwestern accent it was easy to miss how smart he was. He chose his words carefully, sometimes slowly, and this added to his modest demeanor. But as I would soon find out, the modesty ended when his golf clubs started talking.

As we drove to the range, he told me that he had always dreamed of being a professional athlete. He played NAIA Division II basketball in college and even tried out for the Minnesota Twins as a first baseman. Slowly, he began to focus on becoming a professional golfer. When he became disenchanted with his work as a computer engineer, he quit and gave himself five years to accomplish his goal of becoming a PGA golfer.

As we left my car and walked toward the driving range carrying our clubs, Jaacob asked, "How deep is the range here?"

I laughed. "Well, I've never had to worry about that," I said. Then I realized that we might have a problem. The range was set up so that golfers hit balls from both ends. It was a public driving range on one end and the range for a country club on the other end. In other words, the golfers hit balls directly at each other. We looked at the yardage markers and estimated that the golfers at the private driving range were about 350 yards away.

"I should be okay," Jaacob said. "I'm not going to use my long driver. I'll use my playing driver, which doesn't go as far."

I told Jaacob that I wanted to see a typical practice session—how he warmed up, which clubs he hit first, what he worked on. He began by hitting partial shots with a pitching wedge. He told me that in the Austin swing it was essential to keep the wrists relaxed.

"You can't try to control the swing," Jaacob said. "You have to just have faith that it will work. To gain control, you have to give up control." What he had said struck him as funny and he made a puzzled face. "Does that make sense—that you can gain control by giving up control?"

"It's very profound," I said. "I think you could say that's an analogy for life."

"It's very true in this swing," he insisted. "If you try to guide the club, you won't hit it long and it won't be accurate either."

Jaacob took a pitching wedge and set up carefully, placing the blade behind the ball in a precise manner. He swung using only his hands, with about forty-five degrees of movement. The contact sounded crisp and solid. He hit about six balls this way and they sailed about 10 yards. He began hitting balls with more of a weight shift. The ball climbed high and traveled about 100 yards. It seemed that the balls fell more slowly, almost lazily drifting back to the ground. I remembered what Mike had told me about hitting a "parachute shot" in trick-shot demonstrations. The parachute shot had lots of backspin on it, which seemed to hold the ball in the air longer and make it land more softly.

"Most professional golfers have to really stomp on it to get a pitching wedge to go a hundred and thirty-five yards—if they can even hit a wedge that far," Jaacob said. "I'm just cruising. This swing is so much more efficient than what's commonly taught today. Sometimes when I'm playing, I feel sorry for other players because it's so easy for me to hit it farther and straighter than them."

I asked him to hit a 5-iron. Now his swing was warmed up and he was making a full weight shift. When he hit the ball it took off and sailed with a slight draw. I was amazed to see that when the ball hit the ground it had traveled about 200 yards in the air. He was hitting his 5-iron, with limited-flight range balls, farther than the pros.

Now it was time for the driver. He took several practice swings, and I heard the swoosh that his club made. I thought how Mike had once told me that when he fully released the club, "it sounded like a tornado was coming." The swoosh that Jaacob generated was definitely something I hadn't heard before. I noticed that other golfers around us were looking around, wondering where that noise was coming from.

"You can use the swoosh to tell when you're really swinging the club right," he said. "If you aren't relaxed in the wrists, and in your other joints, you don't get the right sound."

Jaacob teed up a ball, lined up his driver behind the ball, and swung. The ball took off and drew sharply—but then straightened out. It kept climbing and hung in the blue sky for what seemed like an eternity. When it touched down, it was way past the farthest marker.

"That's about my typical distance with this driver and range balls," Jaacob said. He pulled a range finder out of his bag and measured it. "That one carried about three hundred fifteen yards."

Jaacob hit a few more balls and some of them went even

farther. I watched the tiny figures at the opposite end of the driving range as they reacted to the balls that were now coming at them from such a great distance. One ball that Jaacob hit went so far it climbed the bank on the other side. I noticed the country club golfers at that end of the range starting to scatter. They must have felt that they were under attack.

"I got kicked out of a driving range for hitting balls over the fence," Jaacob said. "And I've also snapped a driver shaft and cracked a driver head. With this swing you have to be careful, because you're capable of more than you might think."

Sometime later, I went to my home course, Recreation Park Golf Course, with Jaacob, to hit at the driving range. The base of the backstop was 225 yards from our tee, and the screen was about 200 feet tall. On one of my longest drives, I hit a ball that reached the fence on one bounce. Often, in the afternoons, high school kids tried to hit it over the fence. They swing so hard they seem to come out of their shoes. But I never saw one hit it over the fence. And it was a pretty long poke to even hit the net on the fly. I wanted to see if Jaacob could hit one out of the park.

It was late in the day and only a few people were on the range. Behind the backstop, and across the street, and over an expanse of grass, was the Billy Jean King Tennis Center. Jaacob teed up a range ball and let it fly. It tailed off and hit the backstop about 20 feet from the top.

*Jaacob Bowden has the driving distance to fulfill his dream of
playing the PGA tour.*

"I didn't catch that one solid," Jaacob said, teeing up
another ball.

He swung again and this ball tailed off too, but it cleared the
backstop easily.

"I still didn't get it just right," he said, teeing up a third ball.

This time his swing looked more relaxed and the ball sailed
straight, boring through the air like a missile. We both knew

this ball was well over the backstop, and we were a little nervous about where it might have landed. But we didn't hear any breaking glass, so we assumed everything was okay. Jaacob's mission was accomplished and it was time to put away the artillery. I went back to hitting wedges as Jaacob looked on. A few minutes later the course loudspeaker crackled to life: "Attention on the driving range. Someone hit a golf ball into the tennis court across the street. Please keep your balls in the driving range!"

Two guys behind us, who had just arrived, laughed at this announcement. "No one can hit a golf ball that far," one of them said. "You'd have to be superhuman to do that."

It was one thing to be able to hit these long bombs on a driving range that was wide open. I wanted to see what this kind of distance looked like on the golf course. More importantly, I wanted to see what kind of advantage this amazing distance provided. We met a few days later at Lost Canyons Golf Course in Simi Valley, where Jaacob's pursuit of the Austin swing had started ten months ago with lessons from Danny Shauger.

"I wish you could have seen me back then," Jaacob said. "I was happy just to make decent contact. I had only broken eighty once. My average drive was only two hundred twenty-five yards. Now, I'm on most par-five holes in two. I drive some of the greens out here. And I routinely shoot in the seventies. I even broke seventy for the first time with a sixty-nine. It's the swing. What Mike Austin invented is a better swing. I'm telling you, when you get it dialed in, you just line it up and hit it. It goes right where you're aimed."

I told Jaacob I wanted to warm up using his system. So I asked him to explain it again.

"I build the swing one component at a time," he said. "I use the image of the gears in a car—first gear, second, third, fourth and, I guess, fifth."

My automotive background kicked in and I said, "I think you should call fifth gear *overdrive*."

Jaacob liked that.

I set up and used what Jaacob had called first gear. My weight was on my left side and my stance was slightly open. I swung using only my hands, and the ball went only about 20 feet. But even in this small motion you could feel the solid contact when you hit it right.

Second gear included some "tromboning" action of the right arm so that the right elbow comes into the right hip, similar to the way trombone players draw the slide in toward their shoulder.

Third gear took the left arm farther back so that it was parallel to the ground and flattened across the chest. It was important, Jaacob said, to keep the wrists very flexible. I shook the tension out of my wrists and hit another ball. When I hit it from this position with a pitching wedge, the ball sailed about 90 yards with little effort.

Fourth gear included the tilting of the hips that produced the weight shift. I felt I was as far back as I could go now, but Jaacob showed me how the club could be taken to level by letting the shoulder blades slide for extra motion. I had reached the top and, by looking in a mirror, I saw my club was level. It was a pretty sight; I looked like a real golfer. As I hit my short irons from this position, I began to see distances I had never experienced before. My pitching wedge went 120 yards—the distance my 8-iron used to go. However, whenever I tried this swing with my driver, it was a complete disaster. I just couldn't get the right swing path.

"That's the way I learned it too," Jaacob said. "My short irons improved first, then my mid-irons. My driver was the last thing that clicked into place."

Jaacob watched me as I hit balls. Frequently, my wrists were too tense and the ball tended to go right. Other times, the ball went straight but just didn't have much pop to it. But when I got all the motions right, the ball jumped off the club and sailed much farther than I expected.

One motion that I had trouble with was the toss at the top of the swing. Mike taught his students to begin the downswing with a toss of the club. It then caught up with the alignment of the left arm at impact. This was where faith was required. When you gave the club a toss, it felt like you were losing control of it. And, in a sense, you were. This was because you were "releasing the head of the club," as Mike often said. The very meaning of the term "releasing" the clubhead conveyed the feeling of this loss of control.

"I like to think of it as throwing a tether ball around a pole," Jaacob said. "You give it a toss and it turns around the pole on its own. As long as there's no tension in your 'rope,' the tether ball comes back to the same place on its own every time." Later, he showed me a demonstration with the way a door closes. If you got the door swinging with a little push, you could then accelerate it easily with a second push by applying more pressure closer to the hinges. This was leverage in action.

We got in our cart and headed out onto the course. It was late October but scorching hot. The air was so dry it seemed to suck the moisture out of your skin. It was good long-drive weather, though. The first hole was 270 yards from the tees. Jaacob drove the ball onto the fringe with a 3-wood. He chipped expertly to within a foot of the hole and tapped in for a birdie. Meanwhile, I had hit a 3-wood to about 70 yards and a wedge to the back of the green. I luckily rolled the ball to within inches of the hole and tapped in for par.

"You had a tap-in birdie, I had a lucky par," I said. "I guess that's a demonstration of how important distance is. But do you think there is a point at which distance stops being useful?"

"Not as long as your distance is accurate," Jaacob said. "Accurate distance is a huge advantage. Of course you will have to chip and putt and make the short shots too. But with this swing you'll make a lot of two-putt birdies."

"How long are you compared to the guys on the tour?" I
asked as we drove to the next hole.

"Hank Kuehne is the longest, and his average drive is three
hundred and twenty-one yards," he said. "My average is also
three-twenty-one."

"So you're already as long as the longest guy out there,"
I said.

Long, I thought, but how accurate and consistent? I knew
that playing casually, as we were now, was nothing compared
to playing in front of a gallery. Could he handle the pressure? Could he hit the big drive on the eighteenth hole on
a Sunday afternoon with water on the left, a full gallery
holding its breath, and the TV cameras rolling? That was the
real question.

During that round Jaacob hit many long drives in the range of
300 yards, and they were amazingly accurate too. But two drives
really stood out in my mind. On the sixteenth hole we were looking
at the green 280 yards away. But it was way up on the side of a
mountain. And the wind was in our faces. In the distance we could
see two golfers on the green lining up their putts.

"I'm going to really go for this one," Jaacob said.

Feeling the wind on my face, and looking at this vast uphill
distance, I thought *no way*. But I admired the spirit of youth
and ambition. And it also seemed to echo the Mike Austin *go
for broke* attitude. I leaned on my club and waited for Jaacob to
return to reality.

Jaacob went through his preswing routine, slowly feeling the release motion, then enlarging it. He swooshed the club several times. He seemed to be satisfied with the results. He teed up the ball and placed the large head of his Nike driver behind the ball.

I've always been afraid to really swing hard, because when I do, my swing seems to fall to pieces. But I watched as Jaacob swung the club with a speed that seemed impossible for a mortal golfer. And he still finished in a graceful balanced pose. The ball exploded and took off with a crackling sound as it tore through the air. It climbed steadily and held its line, boring through the wind. It was hard to see exactly how far it went. But moments later the two golfers on the green began whooping and jumping around, waving their arms excitedly.

"I guess I'm on the green," Jaacob said. "I hope they're not mad 'cause I hit into them."

"No," I said. "I think they enjoyed it."

When we got up to the green, Jaacob's ball was pin-high, 30 feet from the hole. He had driven it 280 yards uphill into the wind, easily the equivalent of a 320-yard drive.

Jaacob's drive amazed me in several ways. I was surprised that he would even attempt to hit a ball into a strong wind, 280 yards away and up the side of a mountain. But even more incredible was the way he had blended precision with power. Swinging harder didn't make him wild—it seemed to make him more accurate.

The next hole was a 385-yard par-4 that went steeply down-hill from the elevated tee box. We couldn't even see the green from where we were hitting. Jaacob unleashed another big drive and, while it was still in the air, said, "That one's on the dance floor." When we got to the green, we saw his ball was pin-high but on the fringe. He chipped close and made the putt for another birdie.

As I drove away from the golf course, I realized I had seen the closest thing to watching Mike himself hit the ball. And I also experienced, firsthand, how distance may change the way golf is played. I was so excited about this that I had to tell someone what I'd seen. I had my cell phone with me and con-sidered putting in a call to my brother Peter, an avid golfer. I also thought of my friend Louis Lebherz. But then I real-ized that there was only one person who I needed to talk to. And he couldn't be reached by phone. I pulled out my map and began picking out my route to get there.

CHAPTER 17

A LEGEND IN DECLINE

When Mike first broke his hip, I thought his health would decline quickly and he might die within weeks. I even dreaded the idea that I would stumble across an obituary about him in the paper some morning. But Mike bounced back to life time and time again, cheating death. I began to suspect that this was just another phase in Mike's amazing life, a life that would seemingly stretch on forever. One day, while I was playing golf with Lou Lebherz, we speculated that the grim reaper had tried to take Mike, but Mike must have beat the crap out of him and sent him packing.

"He probably punched him so hard his eye fell out of his socket," Lou said, echoing a story Mike once told about a fight he had been in. "The grim reaper decided 'We don't want this guy!' and took off running."

It was fun to joke about this, but once, when I went to visit Mike in the hospital, I realized it was just bravado. No one escapes death, no matter how tough he is. The grim reaper always gets you, because he has time on his side. He has all of eternity, and he just stalks you until you can't fight him off any longer. This was where Mike was—in the final stages of his long fight.

Mike had crashed his plane into a crocodile-infested swamp in Nigeria. He had contracted "Fever X" that killed everyone else who caught it. He had been thrown through a car's windshield and across six lanes of traffic. He had looked down the barrel of a submachine gun while trying to collect a gambling debt. He had come face to face with death so many times he probably thought he would live forever. But it was becoming clear, he would not.

I thought of these things as I drove to see him that afternoon after playing golf with Jaacob. I wanted to tell him that his swing would be immortal and that the freedom that distance brings was a gift he had given to the world of golf. I had so many things I wanted to tell Mike and so many questions left to ask him. The thought that I hadn't wrung the last drop of information about his life from him was haunting me. I knew there were still secrets to learn and stories to tell. Maybe, I was beginning to admit, I would never hear everything he had to tell me about his long, rich life.

The convalescent hospital, where Mike had been moved after his hip operation, was quiet when I arrived. Most of the patients were in their rooms watching TV, reading, or simply lying quietly, neither asleep nor awake, drifting in a world where the past, the present, and the future all mingled together. I asked the nurse at the desk if Mike was alone. She said he was, and it seemed that she brightened up when she realized I was there to see Mike. Apparently he had made some friends here at his new home.

In my visits to see Mike in the hospital I had gained new respect for his amazing spirit. No matter how sick he was, he insisted on being put in his wheelchair and pushed down the hallways. He sat straight up with perfect posture and greeted the other patients warmly. Mike joked with the nurses and doctors and called them all by name. I remember we were passing a man who was slumped over in his wheelchair, barely conscious, but Mike nodded to him and asked, "How are you today, sir?" Anyone else would have pitied this man. Mike reached out and tried to make contact with him, searching for a spark of life inside the shell of old age.

I knocked on Mike's door and heard his clear voice with a hopeful note in it say, "Come in!"

I entered and saw his face light up as he recognized me. The look of happiness on his face nearly broke my heart.

"Hey, hey! How ya doin', buddy?" he said, reaching out for my hand.

I took his hand in both of mine and squeezed it. I said what I always said when I met him, "Mike, you're looking great. You really are." As I said this I couldn't help notice how much weight he had lost over the past two months.

"You always look good," he told me. "You look like you got some sun."

"I played golf today. And I have something to tell you. You know your student Jaacob?"

He nodded.

"I saw him drive three greens that were about three hundred yards."

"Where'd you play?"

"Lost Canyons."

"I don't know that course . . ." his voice trailed off.

"Mike, I think Jaacob is going to be great. And he swings just like you did." I realized then that I had made a mistake. Mike might be on his deathbed, but I imagined he still had that competitive spark in him. There was only one Mike Austin, I reminded myself. But he didn't react jealously to my statement, which I took as a bad sign.

"So how are you feeling?" I asked.

"I'm much better. I want to go home—immediately," he said with a hurt tone in his voice. I was sure he was pushing the doctors to be released.

"I'm sure you will go home soon," I told him. "You know Mike, I was back east a few weeks ago and I met an old friend of yours."

"Who was that?" he asked.

"Chandler Harper. And I talked to him about your world-record drive. I was curious to see how he described it." I studied Mike's face for a reaction.

"Chandler Harper is a hell of a nice fella," Mike said, smiling.

"And let me tell you, his wife is a beautiful woman. Absolutely beautiful."

We talked about the Las Vegas tournament and some of the other golfers he had known on tour. Then I changed the subject.

"I've got more news for you, Mike," I said. I went on to tell him that his memoir had been sold in New York to Carroll & Graf Publishers. It was scheduled to be published the next spring, around Father's Day. Even before I had the words out of my mouth, Mike was beaming with happiness. He seemed to bounce up and down in the bed.

"You have my permission!" he said excitedly, as if I had been asking for his approval. "You have my permission!" he said several times, still smiling. We talked about the book for some time, and the more we discussed it, the more sharply I felt his impending death. Would he be alive to read it? Could he enjoy the recognition I hoped the book would bring him?

Mike was beginning to look tired, so I felt I should go. But I couldn't leave without talking about the subject I knew would excite him the most.

"You know, I'm making progress with your swing, Mike. And I've never hit the ball this well. But I'm not getting it all. I can't relax my hands enough in the hitting area to get the pop I need."

I held my hand out and made the motion he teaches. I saw him flinch.

"Not like that," he said, an edge in his voice. "Look here,

move your hand like this. Not a flapping motion, but one that rotates slightly."

I imitated the motion.

"No. No. Look, get the golf club," he said.

"Golf club?"

"Under the bed," he said, impatiently.

"Mike, there isn't a golf club under there," I said, assuming that he was beginning to lose his grip on reality.

"It's behind the goddamned curtain!"

When he got that tone in his voice, I had to obey. To humor him I looked behind the curtain that separated him from his roommate. Sure enough, a club—a fairway wood—was leaning there. Why did I ever doubt him?

With the golf club in his one good hand and the rest of his ancient body on death's doorstep, Mike raised the club and showed me the correct motion that the hand should make as it comes through the ball. It was almost a flicking motion, Mike said; it was stronger and faster than a slapping motion, because it made better use of more muscles.

"I'll try it," I said. "I'm going to need it to reach my goal."

"Remember what I've told you, and you'll get there," he said, handing me the golf club and sinking back into the bed.

Mike looked completely worn out; the earlier excitement seemed to leave him drained. I said I would have to leave. But somehow my feet weren't making for the door. I realized there

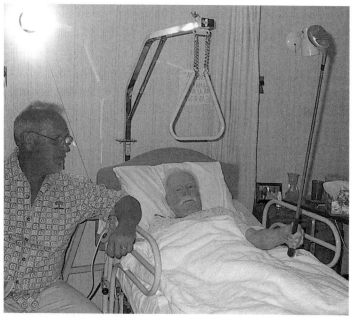

In the hospital Mike kept a club nearby so he could give lessons to opera singer Louis Lebherz.

was something that was bothering me, something I had always wanted to ask him.

"Mike," I said. "I sure hope the book brings you the recognition you deserve."

He frowned and then spoke in the crisp enunciating way of his. "Recognition comes with the truth," he said at last. "Besides, the people who count, they know me. If I went into a hotel lobby, at a tournament or someplace, all the top players came to me to shake my hand. Nicklaus, Palmer, Gary Player, they would all stand up and come over to me, to shake my hand."

That comment was very important to me. It showed that at least on some level he got out of life what he wanted. At that moment, some of the pressure I had put on myself, to tell the world what a great golfer he had been, was lifted. I didn't need to do it for him, since he already felt he had received many of the accolades he deserved. Still, I wanted to understand what he did and to bring it to the millions of golfers searching for a better swing.

Mike closed his eyes and I thought he had fallen asleep. I studied his still-handsome face in profile. He looked calm and detached. I had never seen him this way before, and I had the feeling he was leaving me—had already partially left me. It made me think back to something Louis Lebherz had said. Louis became the musical director of a Catholic church, and as part of his job he sang at many funerals. Once, during a round of golf, Louis told me his work had given him a better under-standing of death.

"Can you describe death to me?" I asked.

He thought it over carefully. Then, in that rich operatic voice, filled with drama, he said, "Death is a thin veil."

"What do you mean?"

"When people die, they don't really leave—at least not right away. They pass through a thin veil. They are there with us for some time. Then, slowly, they leave."

I thought of that now as I looked at Mike's face, the face I was used to seeing so animated, filled with strong emotions. The emotions had cooled now. He was peaceful. He was getting ready to step behind the thin veil.

And now it was time for me to go. I was still at the mercy of life's demands; I needed to beat the traffic, needed to get home to my family, needed to get ready to go to work the next day.

"I have to hit the road, now, Mike," I said.

"Thanks for coming, buddy," he said as I held his hand in both of mine.

"I'll be back," I said.

He gripped my hand tightly, looked into my eyes, and said, "You're a great man." But in his Scottish/Southern accent it sounded like he said, "You're a great *mun*." He added, "Come back any time. And bring your boys with you."

"I will."

I stood at the door and saluted at him. He returned my gesture with a wink.

When I got back to my house, I went for a swim in our pool and cooked burgers on the grill. I went to the golf course at sunset and hit all eight balls onto the green from 137 yards. It was only when I was getting ready for bed that my thoughts returned to Mike.

I thought of Mike lying in the hospital bed in the quiet night. He would be alone now with no visitors to keep him company. I began to wonder what he was thinking about. Or dreaming about. I was pretty sure his mind wasn't dealing with the problems of 2003 such as broken pipes or hospital payments or even the details of his golf instructional book. I suspected that his mind was in the past somewhere, hitting balls while Bobby Jones watched in amazement, or carousing in Hollywood with Errol Flynn. Or perhaps he was flying secret missions to Cairo in a cargo plane. Or maybe he was walking the fairways with Ben Hogan and Sam Snead.

No, I decided, Mike wasn't lonely at all. The past is all around him, ready to welcome him into the ranks of the legends that have preceded him.

Mike Austin played golf with all the legends of his time.

CHAPTER 18

IN THE FOOTSTEPS OF MY HERO

As soon as I arrived at the Desert Rose Golf Course in Las Vegas, I sensed the presence of Mike Austin. This was the first time I had set eyes on the course where he made his record drive on September 25, 1974, while playing in the U.S. National Seniors Open. Ever since I had heard about his feat, I wanted to play here, to stand on the tee box where Mike stood and look down the fairway at the distant green that was unreachable to all other golfers. I wanted to see what it was like to stand behind the ball, driver in hand, and dare to imagine you could blast the ball past the green, 450 yards away. So when my job took me to Las Vegas for a convention, I arranged to leave early and drive there with a friend so I could play a round of golf in the footsteps of my hero.

It had required a bit of detective work just to find the golf course. The Winterwood Golf Course wasn't even listed in the current Las Vegas phone book. Calling around, I learned that the name had been changed to the Desert Rose Golf Club. Furthermore, I discovered that the front and back nines had been

reversed. The fifth hole, where Mike had hit his drive, was now
the fourteenth hole, and it had been lengthened slightly to 455
yards from the tournament tees.

By this juncture, November 4, 2003, I had been in search of
my goal of hitting a 300-yard drive for several years. I had
studied Mike's video and practiced a lot on my own. Recently,
I began even more aggressively to improve by taking lessons
from Danny Shauger. I would then visit with Mike for brush-
up lessons as he sat in his Barcalounger and later his wheelchair, and still later, as he lay in his hospital bed. He would
check my grip, stance, and takeaway with an eye that never
seemed dimmed by age or frailty. My hope was that when I
reached the fourteenth hole on the Desert Rose Golf Course,
where Mike had set the all-time long-drive record, I would
achieve my own much more modest goal, by tapping into whatever mythic force he had used to launch the greatest drive in
history.

As I considered my goal, I realized I was somewhat con-
flicted in my intentions. If I hit my 300-yard drive on the very
same hole where Mike set the record, it would seem almost too
perfect to believe. In my experience, life doesn't provide the
kind of perfection and symmetry we try to impose on it. You
can daydream about how you would like your life to turn out,
but as some sage recommended, "If you want to make God
laugh, tell him your plans." Besides, it didn't really matter what
hole I achieved my goal on—it just mattered that I did it, so I

could prove that Mike's teachings had significantly improved my golf game.

While the 300-yard drive symbolized success, I had to say that Mike's teaching had already greatly improved my accuracy and increased my distance. My length off the tee had gone from an occasional 200-yard drive to a more consistent 250 yards and more. My pitching wedge, which I hit 90 yards when I met him, I could now hit 120 yards. My 5-iron, which used to be so unreliable that I didn't really assign a distance to it, now went 170 yards and dead straight. So I was assured that Mike's method had worked magic with my swing. But, with my longest drive measuring about 270 yards, I still hadn't quite reached the goal I set out to achieve.

It had been a long car trip from Los Angeles to the Desert Rose. When my friend dropped me at the course, my muscles were tight and my back was stiff as I stepped out of the car. I would have to thoroughly stretch to achieve the "supple quickness" Mike said was necessary for good ball striking. Looking around, I saw a modest clubhouse, a low tan building typical of structures in Las Vegas, where temperatures often reach 110 degrees in the summer. Today though, it was sunny and cool with only a slight breeze blowing. Perfect golfing weather.

I carried my clubs through a walkway between the pro shop and the restaurant. Other golfers milled around, excitedly describing the round of golf they had just completed. Or as they prepared to tee off, speculating hopefully about how they would

The Winterwood, renamed the Desert Rose, was one of the first golf courses in Las Vegas.

play that day. Still others paid off bets or negotiated for extra strokes while proposing bets and setting the stakes. I imagined Mike here on that day in September 1974, his spikes rattling on the concrete, joking with other golfers, eyeing the women, and enjoying the excitement of the tournament and competition. He didn't know that later that day he would hit the longest drive ever recorded in a tournament. And he didn't know that thirty years later that record would remain unbroken.

In the unpretentious pro shop, Matt Cradduck, operations manager for the golf course, greeted me warmly as I walked in. He hadn't heard about Mike's record-setting drive until I phoned him a day earlier to reserve a tee time. When Matt heard that history had been set on his course, it seemed to spark his imagination. I chatted with Matt and told him a bit about Mike Austin, how he had always been a long hitter, much longer than anyone else on the tour.

"So how long was this drive?" Matt asked.

"It was five hundred and fifteen yards," I answered. "He hit it on what is now the fourteenth hole. It carried all the way to the fringe and then bounced sixty-five yards past the pin."

Matt nodded, visualizing that hole. "Not to take anything away from him, but when you get out there you'll see that fourteen is a slight dogleg right, so it might be a little shorter. There are trees along the right side, so if you went straight at the green you could cut the corner and . . ." He paused, visualizing the flight of the ball. "How long did you say the drive was?"

"It was five hundred and fifteen yards."

He shook his head in disbelief. "That's one hell of a drive."

"Yes, it is," I said. "That's why I'm here."

Matt advised me to play the back nine first so I would be sure to reach the fourteenth hole before dark. I went out to the range and began to warm up slowly and carefully. I hit chip shots, keeping my wrists loose and feeling the solid contact. I enlarged the swing and, with almost no effort, hit my pitching wedge 90 yards. I knew I should try my driver, but I was hesitant since my drives had been erratic lately. The improvements I had seen with all my other clubs hadn't yet translated to my driver. Would the driver be my friend on this important day? I sure hoped so.

I pulled out my Snake Eyes driver with a regulation-length, regular-flex shaft and eleven degrees of loft on the composite-metal clubhead. I had purchased the individual parts—grip, shaft, and clubhead—for about forty-five dollars and assembled them myself to save money, since many of the well-known brand-name drivers would cost me as much as five hundred dollars. Thinking of this reminded me of how Mike once told me he had modified his clubs himself, even as a teenager. He would hit a shot to feel how much flex the hickory shaft offered, then trim it slightly with a sharp knife before hitting another shot. He sometimes drilled out the clubheads and added lead for more weight and reversed the leather grips so he could play with the suede side toward his hands. When steel shafts were developed and introduced, Sam Snead tried them and found them too stiff. He gave the set of shafts to Mike, telling him, "You're the only player I know who could swing these."

The thirty years between 1974, when Mike set the record, and today has seen a revolution in golf equipment. He hit his drive with a steel-shafted driver with a head made of dense persimmon wood. The face of the drivers back then had hard plastic inserts and the soles often had heavy brass plates. The driver I would be using had an ultralight graphite shaft designed to "kick"—add extra speed—at just the right point in the swing. My driver's head was much larger than the old per-simmon heads but also much lighter, more forgiving (for off-center hits), and more responsive. The balls have become hotter too, with the development of plastics, silicone, and improved rubber, and they are engineered with sophisticated dimple patterns that improve aerodynamics.

I hit a few drives that hooked sharply, diving hard to the left. I swung again, not expecting distance, just letting the swing flow nicely and keeping my wrists relaxed. I looked up to see the ball hanging in the air. It hit hard and ran off the back end of the range. How far would that have traveled on the course? Out here on the range the ground was hard and the ball ran forever. But from where I stood, I could see the tenth hole. The fairway looked soft and lush as if the ball would check up quickly. I hit a few more drives, and each one felt solid and carried far beyond what I expected. I had never hit my driver this well before or felt so confident with this swing.

It was time to head out.

I got into my cart and headed to the tenth tee box. I would be playing solo today, which was a little unusual, but I preferred it under the circumstances, since it would let me concentrate on the task at hand. The tenth hole was a dogleg left across an irrigation ditch. I teed off with a 3-wood, intending to build my confidence. The ball flew too high to carry far, but it landed right in the middle of the fairway at the 150-yard marker. I put a 7-iron on the green and two-putted for a par. I was off to a good start.

On the next hole I found that I had caught the twosome playing in front of me. When they waved me up I made the classic mistake of hurrying all my shots. I took a double bogey. The next hole was a 160-yard par-3. I hit a high 6-iron with a slight draw that checked up nicely. I two-putted and parred the hole. My drive on the next hole was long and straight. But it didn't have the real pop of a great drive. I guessed it was about 245 yards. From this fairway I could look across at the four-teenth hole—running in the opposite direction—which I would be playing next. I felt a flicker of nervousness in my stomach. Maybe this unsettled me, because I sent my approach shot wide of the thirteenth green, chipped poorly, and took a bogey. I moved on to the next hole.

The hole where Mike hit his 515-yard drive.

The tee box for fourteen was near a road carrying heavy afternoon traffic. Beside me, over a chain-link fence, was the parking lot of a discount department store. All around me were stucco-colored condos with small backyards. I doubted that the area had looked anything like this back in 1974. I figured it was still way out in the lonesome desert then. Now, the sprawl of Las Vegas had grown up around it. But some things hadn't changed. Over the tops of the nearby buildings, I could see Sunrise Mountain, the mountain that Chandler Harper had referred to when I interviewed him earlier that summer. He had joked that a gust of wind had blown down off that mountain and helped carry Mike's ball

Chandler Harper mentioned Sunrise Mountain when he recalled Mike's drive.

into the record books. Now, the afternoon sun was bringing out shades of red and brown, and even purple, on the flanks of the mountain.

Mike's wife, Tanya, had said that when Mike hit his drive on this hole, "it was like God had held it up in the air" as it hurtled forward. And that summer, I recalled Mike arguing with Dunaway about the golf swing. "You can't go against God!" he thundered, as if the swing he used was divinely ordained. Standing there on that tee box, thinking about these two references to God's golfing powers, I wondered if a small prayer might not be in order before I tried to achieve my own goal. I reviewed some of Mike's advice and, closing my eyes for a moment, I pictured his beautiful swing, so balanced, so fluid, so graceful.

The 14th hole is long and narrow with a dogleg right.

I teed up my ball and stood behind it, looking down the fairway. In the distance, I could see a striped pole placed in the center of the fairway to show that it was 150 yards from the center of the green, which was 455 yards away. Seeing this, I knew if I hit my ball to the pole I'd have achieved my goal of a 300-yard drive. I took a few practice swings and reminded myself to finish my backswing, to keep my wrists supple, and to stay down through the shot. Then, as I carefully set up beside the ball, I wiped my mind clean and replaced these swing thoughts with the vision of a white ball flying through the air, refusing to fall back to earth.

I took the club back and swung. In the instant between when the ball was struck and when I looked up to see it, my mind registered that the contact was solid. Solid, but not, as they say, dead-solid perfect. Still, when I looked up, the ball was flying dead straight—not hooking or slicing a bit—and it was on a good line, straight at the 150-yard marker. It took one big bounce and ran for about 20 yards. From where I stood, it looked like it was lying right next to the striped 150-yard pole. I jumped in the cart and sped along the edge of the fairway. When I drew next to where the ball had landed, I found that it was barely short of the pole. I paced it off and found that it was 11 yards short of the 150-yard marker. It was my longest drive ever—294 yards. But it was still six yards short of my goal.

Part of me was thinking, *Why couldn't I have hit it just another six more yards!* But another part of me was happy that I had

My longest drive ever still left me over 150 yards to the green.

shattered my previous record of 270 yards. Besides that, I knew that if I could hit it 294 yards, I would certainly hit it over 300 yards sometime in the near future.

The rest of that round was rather anticlimactic. I continued reaching for 300 yards, but I never got as close. However, my drives were long and exceptionally straight. I finished out my round as the last light faded from the sky. Since I had been dropped at the course by a friend, I had to call a cab to get to my hotel. I went out front to wait for the taxi as darkness closed in around the Desert Rose. The final golfers came off the course, put their clubs in their car trunks, and drove away.

The bridge in the distance is where Mike hit his drive from and it bounced over this green.

As the evening became eerily quiet, I reflected on the sharp contrast between the dark, empty golf course behind me and the glowing lights of the Vegas Strip in the distance.

Once again I became overwhelmed with a sense of Mike Austin's presence. I imagined him coming off the course with Chandler Harper and making dinner plans, or maybe picking a show on the Strip to see. The news of the big drive hadn't really dawned on everyone until the Guinness people made it official several days later. But had there been talk of it that night among the foursomes of the tournament? Or was everyone used to Mike's amazing distance by that time? As a researcher and journalist, I wanted to know the answers to these things. But it was so long ago that the details were now lost in often-told stories that had been embellished, enlarged, or even forgotten. I had to satisfy myself with speculation based on my relationship with Mike and Chandler and on the scant information I had dug up through newspapers and record books.

As I waited for the cab, the streetlights came on and the cold of the desert descended on me. To keep myself warm I took my driver out of my bag and swung it, watching my shadow on the ground as I did so. I swung the club again and heard the swoosh it made as it whipped through the air. I remembered Mike's description of his swing, that it sounded "like a tornado coming." My swoosh seemed puny in comparison—more like a summer breeze. But then I followed Mike's advice and held the club just tight enough so it wouldn't fly out of my hands. The gentle swoosh took on a menacing snarl. Still not a tornado, but I was making progress. It was fascinating that this seemingly simple motion—the golf swing—could be filled with such mystery and so much allure.

I was still wondering why my ball went only 294 yards and not the extra 6 yards I needed to break 300. Still, since taking lessons from Mike, I had increased my driving distance by 70 yards. I continued swinging my club, and I began to feel very good as I tried to picture the look on Mike's face when I told him what I had achieved.

The round at the Desert Rose ended right at sunset.

CHAPTER 19

Going Home

A few days before Thanksgiving I called Mike's house, expecting to reach his wife, Tanya. I wanted to see what photographs of Mike's career were available for me to use in his memoir. And I was eager to go to the hospital to tell Mike about my trip to Las Vegas and my round of golf at the Desert Rose. But Tanya didn't answer the phone. Instead, it was answered after the first ring and a strong voice announced, "Mike Austin."

At first, I thought my phone call had been forwarded to his room at the convalescent hospital.

"Mike. Hi, it's Phil Reed."

"Hey, buddy! It's great to hear from you. Are you going to come up for a visit?"

"Yeah, sure. But—where are you?"

"I'm home!" he said. I can't begin to describe the happiness in his voice as he said this. Two simple words, but they held all the joy of the world in them. "I just got home a few minutes ago."

"Mike, you are amazing. I think I lot of people counted you out a long time ago. But you're back."

"I'm back. I'm back home. And let me tell you, it's super."

When I began work on this book, I thought there was a good chance the ending would be about Mike's death. I pictured a touching scene where Mike would say what turned out to be his final words. I imagined my own feelings of losing a friend. And I wondered how it would feel to know that the world had lost a man like Mike. But Mike, who had always upset people's expectations, and had always exceeded everyone else's predictions, did it again. He made it back home one more time.

The next day I drove over to Mike's house to visit him with a very specific purpose in mind. For once, I wanted to talk to him about myself, to tell him how much I had improved, and to describe my trip to Las Vegas and the near-accomplishment of my goal. We had never spent much time talking about me, and I wondered how he would react to my news.

Driving along the freeway, I reflected on some recent improvements to my swing. My 294-yard drive in Las Vegas remained my longest, but I continued increasing my consistency and accuracy as I rewired my muscle memory, using the Austin swing more fluidly. In my most recent two rounds of golf, I had hit six drives in the 250-yard range. Like Mike, I was hitting short irons into the green on many holes. In one case, I was paired with a huge guy who was really belting the

Phil Reed is still chasing his 300-yard goal.

ball. On the sixteenth hole of my local course, he hit a mon-
ster drive that the others in my foursome cheered. Moments
later, I hit my drive on the same line, and from the tee box it
looked like our balls came to rest close to each other. As we
drove down the fairway in our cart, my partner boasted, "Well,

it looks like I got you by about twenty yards!" But when he checked what he thought was his ball, he meekly said, "Oh, I guess this is yours." My drive measured 277 yards. As I pulled up in front of Mike's house, I thought how it was moments like this that I had thirsted for when I began my quest for distance six years ago.

I knocked on the front door, heard voices inside, and entered.

"Is the famous Mike Austin in here?" I called.

"Right in here, buddy!" Mike answered, laughing.

I walked into the living room and found that it had been recarpeted now that all the plumbing problems were repaired. The walls were repainted and many of the pictures had been taken down and put in storage. It was much cleaner and brighter than before. Mike's Barcalounger had been replaced by a motorized hospital bed that allowed him to raise and lower it. Mike was lying in the raised bed, and he hailed me with a wave and a big smile on his face. He looked better than I had seen him look in months. His white hair was neatly cut and combed back, and his eyes seemed to dance with the joy of being back in his own home. Tanya pulled a wheelchair up beside his bed and together we helped Mike into it. As Tanya fixed a cup of what she called "hobo coffee"—heating the grounds in a pot and then straining them out as she poured it—I sat across from Mike on the couch.

"Mike, I want to tell you a golf story," I said. "Do you like stories?"

"Definitely."

"Well, I think you'll really like this one." I told him how when I first met him and asked if he could teach me to hit a 300-yard drive, he had told me that it had nothing to do with size and strength. The key was "supple quickness." He smiled, hearing his own words voiced by someone else. I told him his words gave me the encouragement to improve and reach my goal. Then I told him how I went to Las Vegas and played the Desert Rose, where he had played with Chandler Harper and set the world record. My intention was to fulfill my goal on the same hole that he had clobbered his world-record drive. I paused and asked him if he could describe what the hole looked like.

"It was flat," he said quickly. "And there was a culvert on the right. And to our left was a mountain—they called it Shadow Mountain or something."

"Sunrise Mountain."

"Sunrise—that was it. So what happened?" he asked.

I told him how I knew I had to hit the ball past the 150-yard marker to achieve my goal. He was quiet, listening, waiting to hear if I succeeded.

"I remembered all your advice and I kept everything really smooth," I said. "I knew I hit a good one, and it went straight at the hundred-and-fifty yard marker. But I didn't know if I made it there or not. I jumped in my cart and went tearing up there—and when I got up there it was eleven yards short of the marker. It was two hundred ninety-four yards."

He nodded politely. Then, he said, "You know, that Chandler Harper sure is a nice fella. And let me tell you, he had the best-looking wife."

"Yeah, I know," I said, disappointed at his reaction. I wanted to say, *Mike, wait a second, this is about me for once, okay? So what do you think? Did I do something that was actually worthy of a compliment from you?*

Maybe he didn't understand what I was saying. I leaned forward and decided to really spell it out. "You encouraged me to reach my goal and you helped me do it. I know it wasn't three hundred yards—but two-ninety-four is better than I'd ever done before."

"That's wonderful," he said unenthusiastically.

"I did it because of what you taught me," I said.

"Well, thank you."

We sat there in silence for a few moments. I didn't want to continue to beg for a reaction. But I desperately wanted him to say something else to me. Something that would make me feel I was worthy of his praise. But the words didn't come. He was quiet, probably thinking of Chandler Harper, the beautiful wife, or his own golf accomplishments. And then it hit me: If he praised me it wouldn't be true to his character. It wouldn't be like Mike. I was expecting him to turn into something he wasn't—just for my satisfaction. He didn't encourage anyone with praise. He encouraged them through his own amazing example. He demonstrated what was possible and urged you to live up to it—or try to exceed it.

Then I surprised myself by asking a question I hadn't prepared. The question just jumped out.

"You know, I've always wondered something," I said.

"What's that?" he asked.

"Did you hold back your real secret? Did you hold back the real secret that gave you your distance?"

"I always shared everything I knew," he said, looking away. But then he turned back to me, and his eyes held mine. I thought back to the first time I had met him, when he gave me that appraising stare that seemed to drill right through me. His steady gaze always sparked some discomfort in me. But this time it brought excitement. Mike lowered his voice and spoke confidentially. Maybe this was it. This was the key to take the next step to becoming truly great.

"Once you master the physical motions of the golf swing, distance becomes an activity of the mind," he said.

"In what way?" I sensed something wonderful was about to emerge from the recesses of his amazing mind.

"The speed of the club is activated by a stimulus from the brain. You have to stimulate the nerve that creates the motion of the muscle that bends the joints in the sequence necessary to get into position to hit the ball. But you have to pre-think, understand? You don't think while you're doing it. It has to become a habit."

My first reaction was, *What the hell did all that mean?* But I had been around Mike long enough to know that there was substance in all of his comments. So maybe that was his secret, that he was also more powerful than most in his thinking. I didn't know for sure what it meant, but I was so intrigued by that statement I forgot for a moment about my bruised ego.

"So that's it, then?" I asked. "That's the secret."

He looked directly at me and, very slightly, he nodded.

I felt like a mountain climber who thinks he has reached the summit only to find there is a lot more of the mountain still to scale. I had spent years with Mike, believing I had plumbed the depths of his knowledge. But he had the ability to blow my mind all over again and take me to a still higher plane. I had come here looking for closure to my search for distance. Instead, I was shown the next goal, the next mountain I had to climb.

"Okay, then," I said. "If you pre-think the swing, then what do you think of while you're swinging?"

"I think of the big picture; I think of where I want the ball to go. Then I just leave the rest to my body."

The big picture. Yes, Mike always thought of the big picture. He was a big man, with big dreams, and he had accomplished a lot in his life. But perhaps his greatest accomplishment was helping the people around him, people like me, encouraging them to reach beyond their limitations. My accomplishments sounded insignificant compared to his. But what do you expect when you compare yourself to someone like Mike? He was perhaps the best driver of the golf ball who had ever lived. And I was, well, I was only a pretty good golfer. But what this was really about was not accepting limits, no matter who you are and what limitations you face. Mike was great at not accepting limits. The golf ball he hit seemed to defy the laws of gravity. And here he was, alive and well, sitting in his own home in front of me, defying his doctor's death sentence.

Now I had an invitation not just to swing like Mike, but to think like him too. I had come here hoping for a pat on the back and some closure. But he was encouraging me to continue the journey on my own. I could hit the ball pretty long now, he seemed to say, but how much longer could I become as I improved my mental game and more smoothly blended the motions he taught me? The answer was left for me to discover. I mean, once you've learned the greatest golf swing, who knows how far you can hit it?

My interest in playing golf, rather than just practicing it, has been rekindled now that I've learned Mike's method of striking the ball. With Mike's help I can now play the game at a new level. I go for greens I never dreamed of reaching. I cut doglegs that are protected by trees. I can sometimes putt for eagles on par-5s. But there is nothing I like quite so much as walking down the middle of the fairway after I've hit a good drive. It's an invigorating feeling of anticipation knowing that I'm in great shape for my second shot. If I can get near the hole, it's birdie time. These are feelings Mike felt all of his life, although, I have to say, he was usually putting for eagles, not birdies.

When I recently called Mike he was sitting in his living room with Danny Shauger at his side, planning a trip together to a golf expo in Florida. They would sell their book while sharing a booth with Mike Dunaway, who would be promoting his swing training device. The prospect of the upcoming trip had put Mike in a rare mood. "Come on up and play a round of golf with me and Danny!" he exclaimed, sounding almost giddy with excitement.

"There's nothing I would like better," I answered. And despite relief at his recovery and my satisfaction at learning his swing, I realized there was still one thing I would never do. I would never stand on the tee box beside Mike and see his beautiful, effortless swing—the greatest swing ever—with my own eyes and watch as the ball disappeared into the distance, straight down the middle of the fairway.

Mike Austin's greatest golf swing.

FOR ADDITIONAL INFORMATION

Mike Austin: Secrets from the Game's Longest Hitter; instructional video, www.peacerivergolf.com

How to Kill the Ball: The Mike Austin Method, by Dan Shauger; available through Amazon.com and www.aperfectswing.com

Hit it Hard! The Modern Fundamentals of Power Golf, by Mike Dunaway and John Andrisani, Simon & Schuster, 1992

Free Throw: 7 Steps to Success at the Free Throw Line, by Dr. Tom Amberry with Philip Reed, HarperCollins, 1997

Swing Like a Pro: The Breakthrough Method of Perfecting Your Golf Swing, by Dr. Ralph Mann and Fred Griffin with Guy Yocom, Broadway Books, 1998

LIST OF ILLUSTRATIONS

ACKNOWLEDGMENTS

So many people generously helped me with the research and writing of this book. At the top of the list is Mike Austin himself, and his wife, Tanya. The rest of the people, listed here in alphabetical order, were also essential to the completion of this project:

Dr. Tom Amberry
Jaacob Bowden
Matt Cradduck, operations manager, Desert Rose Golf Club
Mike Dunaway
The executives and editors at Edmunds.com Inc.
Chandler Harper and the staff of the Bide-A-Wee Golf Course, Portsmouth, Virginia
Jay B. Hutchens
Scott Jacobs
Katherine and Jack Lathrop
Louis Lebherz
Phil Lebherz
The Los Angeles Times Magazine
Lost Canyons Golf Course
Bryn MacKinnon
The Mavericks Writers Group
Recreation Park Golf Course
Vivian, Andrew and Tony Reed
Peter and Kevin Reed
Danny Shauger

Martin J. Smith
Brad Swingle
Philip Turner, Editor in Chief, Keith Wallman,
    and the staff of Carroll & Graf Publishers
James A. Ullrich
Robert Wilson, Wilson Media

ABOUT THE AUTHOR

Philip Reed has spent his life writing about three things: sports, cars and crime. He wrote *Free Throw: 7 Steps to Success at the Free Throw Line* with Dr. Tom Amberry, the world's champion free throw shooter. His novel *Ponga Boy* is about a Mexican soccer star and *The Marquis de Fraud* is set in the world of thoroughbred horse racing. His "car noir" thrillers, *Bird Dog* (nominated for the Edgar Award) and *Low Rider*, are about fast cars, fast women, and a reformed car salesman named Harold Dodge. A former newspaper reporter, Phil now works for the consumer automotive Web site Edmunds.com. His nine-part series, *Confessions of a Car Salesman*, was the result of a three month undercover project and can be read on Edmunds.com and AOL. Phil has also written for television and is author of the autobiography *Candidly, Allen Funt*. He lives in Long Beach, California, with his wife, Vivian and his two sons, Andrew and Tony. He is currently an 11 handicap golfer but is planning to go much lower.